JUSTICE FOR ALL?

JUSTICE FOR ALL?

Jews and Arabs in the Israeli Criminal Justice System

ARYE RATTNER
AND GIDEON FISHMAN

Simon Hakim, Advisory Editor

PRAEGER

Westport, Connecticut
London

Library of Congress Cataloging-in-Publication Data

Rattner, Arye.
Justice for all? : Jews and Arabs in the Israeli criminal justice system / Arye Rattner and Gideon Fishman.
p. cm.
Includes bibliographical references and index.
ISBN 0-275-95908-2 (alk. paper)
1. Criminal justice, Administration of—Israel. 2. Discrimination in criminal justice administration—Israel. 3. Palestinian Arabs—Civil rights—Israel. 4. Jewish-Arab relations. I. Fishman, Gideon, 1945– . II. Title.
HV9960.I75R37 1998
364.95694—dc21 98-10075

British Library Cataloguing in Publication Data is available.

Library of Congress Card Number: 98-10075
ISBN: 0-275-95908-2

First published in 1998

Praeger Publishers, 88 Post Road West, Westport, CT 06881
An imprint of Greenwood Publishing Group, Inc.

Printed in the United States of America

The paper used in this book complies with the Permanent Paper Standard issued by the National Information Standards Organization (Z39.48-1984).

10 9 8 7 6 5 4 3 2 1

Contents

Preface

As Israeli social science scholars specializing in criminology, we find it highly tempting to take advantage of the unique social laboratory presented by Israeli society. Living and working in this dynamic society, one that is forever undergoing rapid social change and so deeply influenced by its unique geopolitical situation, we were more than curious to find out how Israel treats its most significant minority group; namely, the Arabs. It is perhaps noteworthy as devoted advocates of the rule of law and strong supporters of human and civil rights, we consider it important and only natural that actions taken by the government and its agencies undergo critical scrutiny. At the same time, we see ourselves as ardent Zionists who believe in the importance and viability of the state of Israel as a Jewish homeland. However, this position should not juxtapose the concern with minority rights issues.

Social concerns like these were also responsible for triggering our previous research into areas such as social stereotyping, sentencing, and attitudes towards the law in Israeli society. In this book, we attempt to explore whether the Israeli justice system dispenses justice equally, irrespective of social grouping. To this end, we examined judicial decisions from the stage of police apprehension through sentencing.

The Israeli justice system, and especially the Supreme Court, enjoy a high level of trust and respect by Jews and Arabs alike. The justice system provides recourse and remedy in the face of personal and public wrongs. In the court of law, the individual citizen, regardless of social status or ethnic group, can face the system as an equal. Thus, if the criminal justice system and the legal system as a whole is to serve as the ultimate shield for the "underdog" in a democratic society, surely its practices should be subject to "watchdog" scrutiny.

Israel is celebrating its fiftieth anniversary as an independent state. Ever since its establishment, Israeli society has suffered many internal conflicts which, at times, have threatened to disrupt the normal course of life. Some of these conflicts, such as the tensions between Ashkenazi and Sephardi Jews, newcomers and old-timers, and the political left and right, will eventually fade away or become existentially insignificant. On the other hand, it is difficult to predict the course of the tensions between Israel's Jewish and Arab citizens as we head towards a time of peacemaking, the results of which are also very uncertain. Arabs have been living in the region for many generations, long before the state of Israel was established. They are culturally and emotionally attached to the land. The creation of the state of Israel as a homeland for the Jewish people in the aftermath of the Holocaust also formalized the national minority status of Arabs in Israel. Demographers forecast that by the end of the millennium, Israeli Arabs will constitute about 20 percent of the country's population.

During the second half of the twentieth century, civil rights and the rights of minorities have featured prominently on the world agenda. In this respect, Israel, which was established largely due to the racial persecution suffered by the Jewish people throughout its two thousand years of exile is, and should be, extremely sensitive to the rights of its minorities. On the other hand, Israel has suffered constant hostility at the hands of its Arab neighbors ever since its inception. The tensions rooted in the Arab-Israeli conflict have inevitably spilled over into the internal relations between Israel's Jewish majority and Arab minority. Thus, the declared intention to treat Arabs fairly and equally has all too often been overshadowed by political tension and existential fear. Despite legislative efforts to protect minority rights and treat all citizens as equals, the results of our study show that such goals are not always achieved.

We do not live in a social vacuum, nor do we pretend to be socially or politically naive. On the basis of preliminary research, we assumed that differential treatment by the justice system and discrimination against Israeli Arabs does exist. What we wanted to ascertain was whether this assumption was correct. This was to be accomplished by examining decisions at each juncture of the criminal justice system.

As liberals in our outlook, we secretly hoped that our findings would come out in favor of the system by showing that, on the whole, it was blind to nationality. As scholars and researchers, we realized that whatever our results, they were likely to bear strong and important social messages.

We examined each stage of the criminal justice process very carefully, aware of the social responsibility that we had taken upon ourselves in view of the potentially volatile nature of the subject. We took extra pains for our work to be methodologically sound and its interpretation level headed so that, whatever the findings, they would be valid and meaningful, untainted by political or social ideology.

The research and writing of this book took over three years. It is the most comprehensive study of this subject ever to be conducted in Israel. We began with a pool of one hundred thousand police files covering a period of thirteen years, from 1980 to 1992. These were later reduced to form a core data base of about sixty thousand cases. To avoid arriving at overly hasty conclusions, a long list of variables, legal and extralegal, were checked for their effects. We desisted from sporadic and unsystematic comparisons of isolated cases, and avoided celebrated court cases appearing in the media. Such material would hardly be representative, nor would it be of much value in attempting to arrive at a generalized, overall view and understanding of prevailing trends in the Israeli justice system. The fact that our findings are based on a very large population, over an extended period of time, provides highly significant statistical and substantive results.

We found that Arabs are treated differentially in the criminal justice system. They are not treated as equals. This, however, is not to suggest (since it is not part of our research design) that police officers, prosecutors, or judges operate on the basis of personal outlook or whim or any explicit instructive policy aimed at discriminating against Arabs. The findings of this study need to be placed in a broader framework which takes into account the political and sociocultural context as well. Public opinion surveys consistently bear witness to the existence of stereotypes, according to which Arabs are portrayed as more violent and dangerous than Jews. Furthermore, such surveys also show that many Israelis seem to be of the opinion that Arabs should be denied fundamental civil rights, such as participation in the election of the prime minister, due to "lack of loyalty" and "conflict of interest." It appears reasonable to assume that, to some extent, the criminal justice system mirrors society, its values and beliefs, including stereotypes. This in itself might account for the differential treatment of Arabs versus Jews by the system. It is imperative that the entire justice system and especially the judiciary, be more aware of any such trend and take steps to ensure that it becomes less of a reflection of prevailing prejudices and stereotypes and more of a leader and shaper of progressive values—gatekeeper of the values that form the moral foundation of the state of Israel, so eloquently stated in its Declaration of Independence.

The writing of this book has been a three-year endeavor and both authors have contributed equally to the whole project. We are indebted to many good people who have helped us. However, we assume sole responsibility for any mistakes or errors. We would like to thank Super Intendent Eli Hertz from the Israeli Police Headquarters in Jerusalem who, in addition to being instrumental in providing us with a workable data set, gave us invaluable assistance and advice to help us become thoroughly familiar with the content and structure of the set. We would also like to thank Mr. Nadav Azulay, head computer support specialist of the Faculty of Social Sciences at the University of Haifa, whose skillful assistance, goodwill, and patience made it possible for us to overcome the many technical problems that arose during the data analysis stage. Thanks also to the administrative head of the Faculty of Social Science, Mrs. Shoshi Landman; the research authority of the University of Haifa; and the chairman of the Department of Sociology, Professor Zvi Sobel for their generous financial and administrative help. Thanks are due to our excellent editor, Mrs. Maya Landau whose professional work and constructive criticism are very much appreciated. We are also grateful to Mrs. Yael Koresh for her help with the final stage of the manuscript preparation, and Mrs. Shoshi Mansfeld for her help with the graphic work. And, last but not least, a special acknowledgment and warm thanks to Professor Simon Dinitz from Ohio State University, our dearest friend, colleague, and mentor who, while on sabbatical at Haifa, spent much time and effort reviewing our manuscript and making many insightful suggestions which greatly contributed to the clarity of presentation and the analysis, and improved the overall quality of the manuscript.

Arye Rattner and Gideon Fishman

1

Israeli Society

INTRODUCTION

Many modern nations have attracted immigrants and large racial or ethnic minorities to their shores, but Israel is probably unique in that the ingathering of exiles from all four corners of the world has been one of its top priorities and a primary goal. The November 1947 United Nations resolution to partition British Palestine between the Jews and the Arabs, and the establishment of the independent state of Israel in May 1948, marked the end of two thousand years of exile for the Jewish people. It also marked the beginning of an unprecedented, almost miraculous, process of nation building—from a community of 600,000 Jews in 1948 to a nation of more than 5.8 million in 1997.

Modern Zionism emerged at the turn of the century. The political orientations of the founders of the Zionist movement were diverse. For many of them, Zionism and the repatriation of the Jews to their historical homeland represented the answer to the many years of anti-Semitic persecution in the Diaspora. Indeed the strong desire, and even the right, to immigrate to Zion was considered axiomatic to the spirit of Zionism.

Small groups of Jewish idealists began migrating from Eastern European countries (Russia, Poland, Rumania) to the ancestral homeland as early as 1882. Jewish immigration to Palestine (and later to the independent state of Israel) was called "Aliyah" (Hebrew word for *ascent*). The various waves of "Aliyah" are usually defined according to period of immigration and country of origin. Five waves of immigration between 1882 and 1948 brought a total of 527,000 Jewish immigrants to Palestine in the pre state period. After the establishment of the state of Israel in 1948, the massive waves of immigration consisted mainly of refugees, many coming simply because there was no place else to go. The 211 percent increase in the Jewish population, from 649,700 in 1948 to 2,115,600 in 1964, was due mainly to the migratory balance (68%) rather than natural increase (32%).

During the pre-statehood years, 89.6 percent of the immigrants were from Europe and America, and only 10.4 percent from Asia and North Africa. During the years 1948–1962, only 45.4 percent were from Europe and America, and 54.6 percent were from Asia and North Africa. During Israel's first sixteen years, 14.6 percent of the immigrants came from Rumania, 13 percent from Poland, 13.3 percent from Iraq, 12.8 percent from Morocco and Tangier, 5.2 percent from Yemen, 4.5 percent from Algeria and Tunis, and the remainder from various other countries all over the world. Although, in the Diaspora, these immigrants had been identified as Jews, in Israel they instantly became Moroccans, Yemenites, Russians or Anglo-Saxons. Very soon, a clear distinction was created between Jews of European origin (Ashkenazi) and Jews of Asian-African origin (Sephardi). However, the cultural tone of the developing young state was predominantly western due to the influence of the early Ashkenazi immigrants. Indeed, concern was expressed by them that the influx of Sephardi Jews with their eastern (Asian, North African) culture would undermine the modern orientation of the new nation. The ethnic and cultural diversity of the two groups soon created a deep ethnic cleavage—a cleavage which was to dominate social relations for years to come.

The inequalities that emerged in the young state were rooted not only in Jewish ethnic diversity, but also in the national identities of its population: In 1948, some 13.6 percent of the population was non-Jewish, mostly Arab. This minority group included Moslems (70%), Christians (21%), and Druze (9%). Today, Israel's Arab minority constitutes 19.3 percent of the country's population. Arab Moslems in Israel, like the majority of Moslems in the world, are mainly Sunis with a minority of Shi'ites. Among the Moslems, there also exists a group of semi-nomadic Bedouins, many of whom now live in permanent settlements in various parts of the country.

Two main factors have played an important role in the status of the Arabs in Israel. By declaring itself to be the homeland of the Jewish nation, and despite the fact that in its Declaration of Independence equal rights were promised to all citizens regardless of religion, race, or gender, non-Jews (and especially Arabs) found themselves discriminated against in many spheres. Arabs whose families had been living in Palestine for many generations suddenly became a national minority in the new independent Jewish state. Moreover, following the War of Independence, which broke out between Israel and the surrounding Arab countries after the Declaration of Independence, Israeli Arabs came to be perceived as "enemies" and as a potential fifth column. As if the demographic diversity were not sufficient to create a stream of social problems, yet another dimension of conflict emerged, one related to the Jewish nature of the state. The perennial question of how Jewish the state ought to be has been a constant bone of contention between the various streams of Judaism and continues to add to the complexity of life in Israel. The question of the Jewish-religious character of the modern state and the relation between state and religion have been painful issues from the beginning. The orthodoxy have consistently opposed trends towards secularization, and non-religious citizens, who constitute 80 percent of the Jewish population, have been hard put to persuade the orthodoxy that those who choose not to observe religious dictates are not necessarily sinners; hence, the ongoing battle against attempts to impose religious rulings on the entire population.

Thus, already in its formative years, the young nation found itself immersed in problems emanating from three deep cleavages—the national conflict (Jewish-Arab), the ethnic conflict (Ashkenazi-Sephardi), and the religious conflict (orthodox-secular).

On the whole, despite the existence of diverse ethnic elements, Israel has succeeded in avoiding the kind of interethnic upheavals that other countries, such as the United States, have experienced. However, the tensions between Israel and its neighboring Arab countries have had a marked effect on the relationship between Jews and Arabs within the state of Israel. Measures taken to promote and safeguard the Zionist dream for the Jewish population have often impinged on the civil rights of the Arab population (e.g., the imposition of military government, limitations on Arab freedom of movement, land confiscation for security purposes, lower budgetary allocations for Arab municipalities). The fact that Israel's Arabs have had equal civic rights from the beginning, only served to amplify the sense of injustice in the face of discriminatory policies and practices.

In this book, an attempt is made to provide answers long overdue regarding the extent to which the Israeli criminal justice system discriminates between the country's two main national groups—the Jews and the Arabs.

SOCIOHISTORICAL BACKGROUND

> And I charged you judges at that time saying: "Hear the causes between your brethren, and judge righteously between a man and his brother, and the stranger that is with him." (Deuteronomy I, 12)

This address by God to the people of Israel clearly teaches us that justice and discrimination were already very important issues four thousand years ago, in this very region. The care taken by Israelite laws to protect strangers in their midst, and the attempt to administer justice equally for Israelites as well as resident aliens, had no parallel in either Babylon or any of the other developed cultures of that time. Thousands of years later, in May 1948, it was this very same principle that guided the authors of Israel's Declaration of Independence to state specifically that equality before the law would be ensured for one and all in the new state. "The state of Israel . . . will be based on freedom, justice, and peace as envisaged by the prophets of Israel. It will grant complete equality of social and political rights to all its inhabitants irrespective of religion, race, or sex" (Declaration of Independence, 1948). The extent to which the tradition of "justice for all" has been followed by the criminal justice system in Israel is the main concern of the study presented in this book.

Although the issue of justice became a concern almost four thousand years ago, crime in the modern Jewish land was a relatively rare phenomenon in its early days, and hardly a cause for alarm. Chaim Nachman Bialik, one of the country's earliest and most prominent modern Hebrew poets, upon immigrating to Israel from Russia in 1924, was caught by surprise when learning about the "first Jewish thief." There are no compilations of crime statistics from the pre-statehood period for comparison but data retrieved from archives (Schmeltz and Salzman 1962;1964) confirm that the criminality of the Jews in Palestine during the period of the British mandate (1918–1948) was negligible by today's standards. This observation is hardly surprising considering the composition of the Jewish population at that time and the select character of the early immigrants and pioneers who immigrated to Palestine in order to fulfill their dreams about Zion. The first waves of immigration during the 1920s and 1930s came from highly ideological movements, in which the formation of ideologies preceded the actual migration and then guided the initial stages of settlement in the new country. The pioneering ideology energized most of the settlers in those days. The establishment of the first agricultural settlements, later to become the first townships, was the primary concern of the early pioneers and, for them, symbolized the rejuvenation of the Jews in their ancestral home. Analysis of the court records, the only crime data source available at that time, indicated that the crime rate (for all types of offenses for the total population) was 7.1 in the Jewish sector and 13.8 in the Arab sector.

ISRAEL AS A MULTICLEAVAGE SOCIETY: IMMIGRATION AND THE ETHNIC CLEAVAGE

The establishment of Israel as an independent state brought about a dramatic change in the size and composition of the population. During the first three years of statehood, 684,000 Jews came to the country, doubling the pre state population. From 1952 to 1954, there was a decline in immigration due to austerity measures and a selective immigrant support policy adopted by the government in its attempt to deal with its failing economy. In addition, some Eastern European governments had imposed restrictions on Jewish emigration, forcing Jews to remain behind the "Iron Curtain" against their will. During this period, less than forty thousand immigrants came to Israel. From 1955 on, Jews began pouring into the country bringing in twenty to seventy thousand immigrants each year for the next ten years. In 1964, there was another decline, lasting about three years before picking up again after the Six-Day War in 1967. All in all, 1,850,000 Jewish immigrants were absorbed during the first twenty years of statehood, an enormous number given the fact that there were only 650,000 Jews living in Israel at the time of its establishment in 1948. By 1967, the Jewish population of Israel was approximately 2.5 million.

The sheer dimensions and wide diversity of these mass waves of immigration, with Jews coming from more than fifty countries, made it impossible for the young country to absorb all the immigrants in the same relatively painless way experienced by the early immigrants. For the first time, the immigration included large numbers of Sephardi Jews from Asia and North Africa whose historical, cultural, educational, and motivational background, even physical appearance, differed distinctly from that of the European Ashkenazi Jews. For most Sephardi Jews, immigration to Israel meant transition from a mainly tradition-bound way of life, to a modern, western-oriented society. As late as 1967, one in six Sephardi families consisted of seven or more members, as opposed to only one in a hundred among Ashkenazi families. Prior to 1967, 56 percent of the Sephardi females over the age of fourteen were illiterate at the time of their immigration (in 1967, this proportion was slightly less but still as high as 44%). For Sephardi males, the illiteracy rate was 26 percent prior to 1967 (18% in 1967). Low levels of education and large family size translated directly into relatively low income. In 1960, the average per capita income of Sephardi families was 48 percent than that of Ashkenazi families.

The gaps between the Ashkenazi and Sephardi Jews have narrowed over the years, though not necessarily at the same rate in each component. Nevertheless, they have not been totally eradicated and are still very much in evidence to this day, with Sephardi Jews continuing to climb the socioeconomic ladder at a much slower pace than their Ashkenazi counterparts.

Government policy in the 1950s and 1960s to settle many of the Sephardi immigrants in peripheral areas served only to exacerbate the problem. These new settlement areas, called development towns, lacked the infrastructure and the resources to absorb large groups of new immigrants. Lack of economic and industrial opportunities created large pockets of unemployment. The educational system was ill-equipped for the task of preparing students for participation in the labor force. High school dropout rates became endemic, resulting in growing despair in both the parental generation and among the young. With increasing rates of unemployment, lower levels of education, and poor housing conditions, these communities soon came to be plagued by high crime rates and other related social problems.

The main opportunity for upward mobility has been the school system. Increasing rates of participation by Sephardi Jews at all levels of education have gradually led to the narrowing of the differentials between them and Ashkenazi Jews. The association between ethnicity and school failure led the authorities to adopt policies to raise the achievement level of Sephardi children. The narrowing of this gap during the 1970s and 1980s reflected large-scale effort by the government to incorporate more Sephardi Jews into the educational system. Integration programs were designed to bring together children of lower socioeconomic status and those of higher status. Reforms were introduced (mainly at the junior high level) aimed at lowering the school dropout rate, even at the risk of lowering the overall quality and level of the education provided. It took until the 1980s for the participation rate of children of Sephardi origin in the ninth grade of high school to become almost equal to that of children of Ashkenazi origin. However, although the disparity in number of years of schooling has decreased, the achievements of Ashkenazi children are still higher than their Sephardi counterparts. In 1991 among persons aged fifteen and over, 21.4 percent of the Sephardi Jews had only five to eight years of schooling, whereas among Ashkenazi Jews only 5.4 percent were at this level (Central Bureau of Statistics 1992). Larger gaps are observed in their rate of participation in higher education. Towards the end of the 1960s, only 2.5 percent of all Israeli-born Sephardi Jews aged twenty to twenty-nine attended institutions of higher education, as compared to 12.6 percent among their Ashkenazi counterparts. These gaps are carried over into the 1990s, when among those who were born to Ashkenazi families 24.1 percent had between thirteen to fifteen years of schooling, compared to only 10.7 percent among members of Sephardi families. The gaps are even larger as we go up the ladder and notice that only 5 percent of Sephardic Jews had sixteen or more years of schooling, while among the Ashkenazi Jews only 24.6 percent had reached this level of education.

Although the relative disparity between the Ashkenazi and Sephardi seems to have decreased, the absolute gap has stabilized and, on some dimensions, continues to grow. This is especially evident when the gap is examined along the income dimension. During the 1980s, income discrepancies increased to the point that the average income of Sephardi families was 80 percent lower than that of Ashkenazi families. The distribution of income, especially in the upper and lower margins, still points at a wide gap: less than 10 percent of those in the top percentile of the income distribution of the total population are of Sephardi origin, and about 75 percent of those in the lowest percentile are of Sephardi origin. If inequality has diminished along the years, it has taken place mainly in the center.

ORTHODOX AND SECULAR JEWS—THE RELIGIOUS CLEAVAGE

The seeds of the religious cleavage were planted as early as the turn of the century when the establishment of a Jewish homeland was but a distant dream. Although religion had played a central role in the preservation of the Jewish nation in the Diaspora, the early Zionists, many of whom were ardent socialists, saw religion as pertaining solely to life in the Diaspora—in the new Jewish homeland, a secular society would be established. Nevertheless, Jewish religious symbols took their place in the emerging culture of the new Israeli society.

The discourse on the status of religion has centered around three main issues. The first relates to the conflict between the principles of a democratic society and the laws of the Torah. Orthodox Jews see religious rulings as taking precedence over legislative and judicial rulings. Their disregard for the rule of law is evident not only in their beliefs, but also in their actions. The second issue relates to the conflict that has arisen due to intolerance on the part of the orthodox community towards secular Jews and their way of life. According to a "status quo" agreement reached with Ben Gurion (Israel's first prime minister), the orthodox community formally relinquished its demand to impose religious rulings in all spheres of life except for some matters related to personal and family status such as marriage and divorce. To this day, these matters are controlled by strict religious laws administered and enforced by the rabbinate. The third area of conflict relates to the demand by orthodox circles that some of their special needs be met, such as exemption from military service, special budgetary allocations for their religious school system, as well as other issues on which consensus has never been achieved between the orthodox and secular members of Israeli society.

Despite the formal "status quo" agreement, the conflict between the two camps has only deepened over the years. The orthodox camp persist in its endeavor to strengthen the link between state and religion. Their declared aim is that religious laws and rules should apply to the entire nation and take precedence over rulings and decisions made by the democratically elected legislature and the judicial system.

The religious-secular cleavage has spearheaded in two directions (both stemming from the same religious beliefs and ideology). The first involves domestic issues related to the definition of Jewish identity and the Jewish character of the state. This has been manifested in relentless attempts, via political deals and manipulations (with religious parties often in a position to tip the political balance) to impose religious rules (by changing municipal bylaws, etc.). The second direction involves extreme national-religious and orthodox elements among the Jewish settlers in the occupied territories who, in many instances, have taken the law into their own hands and acted as vigilantes against Palestinians (e.g., the Jewish underground formed by members of extreme right wing organizations responsible for planting bombs aimed against several Arab mayors). Elements such as these believe that their actions are sanctioned by religious laws, that loyalty to such laws is more binding than loyalty to the laws of the state and, therefore, they should be treated more leniently by the legal system when caught and brought to justice. Indeed, it was an ideological mode such as this that in November 1996 led to the assassination of Prime Minister Yitzhak Rabin by an orthodox extremist acting "in the name of God," claiming that Rabin was a traitor because he was willing to give away parts of "the land" in return for peace with the Arabs. The assassination of a prime minister who was negotiating peace was a clear message to other acting politicians that the radical right wing extremists that many of its members are religious nationalists, will consider giving up land for peace as an act of treason which might bring about grave consequences.

We have expanded our discussion on the religious secular conflict because in the last three decades, since the occupation of Arab land during the course of the Six-Day War in 1967, nationalistic elements have attempted to fill it up with a somewhat different content. Issues related to the borders of the state of Israel and the return of land became central to many members of the national religious camp, and thus also became a part of the debate between orthodox and non orthodox. In a very direct way this has been related to the legal rights and status of both Israeli Arabs and Palestinians, which is the central focus of this volume.

JEWS AND ARABS —TWO NATIONALITIES RESIDING IN ONE STATE: THE NATIONAL CLEAVAGE

Tensions and violence between Jews and Arabs have been part and parcel of the geopolitical scenario of the Middle East ever since the turn of the century, when the forefathers of Zionism initiated Jewish settlement in Palestine. The persecution of Jews in Europe by the Nazis after the rise of Hitler in 1933 resulted in a wave of immigration to Palestine, and formed the background of a new and more violent stage of the dispute between the two nations. Palestinian Arabs, incensed by Jewish immigration and the Zionist movement, accused Jews of trying to invade sites holy to Islam. This led to the outbreak of serious riots in Palestine and massacres resulting in 133 Jews and 116 Arabs dead.

With the Declaration of Independence on May 14, 1948, Israel extended a hand of peace to its Arab neighbors. The response was a full-scale war: five Arab nations—Egypt, Syria, Jordan, Lebanon, and Iraq—invaded the newborn state. By early 1949, after signing armistices with the defeated Arab armies, Israel entered its first phase as an independent state with a population of 650,000 Jews and 156,000 Arabs, all of whom automatically became Israeli citizens. Israeli Arabs became the largest non-Jewish minority group living alongside the Jewish population. The Arab citizens of Israel now comprise 19.3 percent (1,122,000) of the 5.8 million population, their population growth over the past forty-eight years due, first and foremost, to their high birthrate.

From the very beginning, Israeli Arabs have enjoyed the right to participate in the democratic process in that they can vote and be elected to political office. On the other hand, for many years they were subjected to military rule rationalized by security considerations. This was clearly in breach of the democratic values promulgated by the Jewish state. The dualism between legitimate concerns for security and the rule of law within a democratic framework has been evident throughout the history of the State. Military rule imposed on areas inhabited by Arabs limited their freedom of movement between these areas and movement to other parts of the country. This situation persisted until 1966 when the military rule was rescinded.

Israeli Arabs occupy low positions on all economic, educational, and health indexes in comparison to the Jewish population. This, in part, is a consequence of the ecological distribution of the population: Jews live mainly in modern urban areas, whereas most Israeli Arabs live in rural communities away from the major urban centers. It was inevitable, given their minority status and the ongoing war between Israel and its Arab neighbors, that Israeli Arabs would find it difficult to identify with the norms, laws, and legal institutions of the Jewish state and its primary goal to provide a homeland for the Jewish people. Another issue that contributed to the tension between Jews and Arabs revolved around Arab land and property holdings. Those Arabs who were cut off from their holdings during the fighting in 1948–1949 (War of Independence) were declared absentees and had their properties expropriated and transferred to the Custodian of Absentees. Other holdings were confiscated by the government for military and security reasons (such as proximity to the borders of a neighboring Arab state).

The segregation of Arabs from the Jewish population and their inferior civic status inevitably gave rise to mutually negative attitudes. The two sectors lived together but apart, in a way that has been defined as institutional pluralism (Horowitz and Lisak 1989).

In June 1967, in response to threats by Egypt backed by Jordan and Syria, Israel launched a preemptive attack against Egypt, which resulted in a quick and stunning victory over the three Arab countries, and to the occupation of territories more than three times the size of the state of Israel. The 1967 Six-Day War had a profound impact on many aspects of Israeli society. The occupation of the territories, and the West Bank in particular, held religious and historical meaning for many Jews, provoking debate, often heated, regarding the legitimate borders of the State.

The outcomes of the 1967 war also had repercussions on Israel's Arab population, providing the opportunity to restore contact with Palestinian brethren across the borders which, in turn, sharpened and crystallized problems surrounding their dual identity. Despite their Israeli citizenship, many of them became more and more cognizant of the Palestinian identity they shared with their brethren in the occupied territories. This split identity represented a difficult, if not impossible, dilemma for many of them—full identification as Israeli citizens versus full adoption of a Palestinian-Arab identity. This dilemma, resulting mainly from the fact of their residence in a Jewish state, has led to radicalization among many Israeli Arabs. This dual identity cum dual loyalty is reflected in all areas of Arab life in Israel, including crime and the involvement of Arabs in the criminal justice process. This and more, the Six-Day War with the occupation of the territories, and the attempts of Jews to resettle in some of the occupied territories as well as in East Jerusalem had its impact in the legal arena as well. This is perhaps best exemplified by the *Bourkan* case[1] which concerned the reconstruction of the Jewish quarter in the old city of Jerusalem, where Jews lived before they were expelled by the Jordanians during the course of the War of Independence in 1948. After the old city of Jerusalem was taken by Israel in the 1967 Six-Day War, Arab residents were evacuated from their premises, and the old Jewish quarter was reconstructed. Houses and apartments were sold by a public company that was in charge of the reconstruction. The petitioner, Bourkan, who was evacuated from his own house, applied to purchase a house, but his application was rejected. In his petition to the Israel Supreme Court he argued that the criteria adopted by the housing company discriminated against Arabs and were invalid. The defense counsel for the housing company made it clear in court that indeed the intention of the company was to restrict housing in the Jewish quarter to Jews only. The Supreme Court decision refused to interfere, stating that the decision to house Jews in this area was not flawed. That the attorney general of Israel has stated clearly his refusal to extend the Bourkan decision beyond its specific context has distinctly marked the concern of discriminating between equals. The relevancy of the Palestinian problem to the issue of crime and the criminal justice system will be discussed in greater detail in chapter 6.

The problem of crime and societal responses to crime cannot be understood outside the social context. Acts that are considered criminal, and acts that become decriminalized, are time-bound; they are also bound by the status of the perpetrators and the victims. There have been no few incidents of leniency when acts that are clearly criminal are perpetrated by Jews against Arabs. For instance, most of the members of the Jewish underground organization acting against Palestinians who were convicted for murder and other serious offenses and sentenced to lengthy prison terms in 1984 were released as a result of a presidential pardon. When the status of the actors is reversed, the perpetrator an Arab and the victim a Jew, treatment by the judicial system is inevitably much harsher.

This volume explores the functioning of the criminal justice system in the context of the volatile relationship between Jews and Arabs in Israel, and the thirty-year conflict between Jews and the Palestinians of the occupied territories. Our working hypothesis: that the geopolitical situation has a significant impact on the way justice is dispensed and that varying degrees of discrimination are to be found in each stage of the judicial process. The British Prime Minister, Winston Churchill, once said that the nature of a society is revealed by the way it treats its prisoners. On the basis of this observation, let us suggest that the nature of a society is measured by the degree of impartiality of its criminal justice system.

THE LEGAL SYSTEM AND CRIMINAL LAW IN ISRAEL: A CONSTITUTIONAL SYSTEM WITHOUT CONSTITUTION

Largely due to the heritage of the British mandatory administration in Palestine, the principles underlying Israel's criminal justice system are basically in harmony with those of the Anglo-American legal system. In order to render the English legal system intelligible to the native populations of territories held overseas, the former Colonial Office in London prepared a model penal code. This code was promulgated in Palestine in 1936 as the Criminal Code Ordinance. The current penal code (Penal Code 1977) is a modified, modern, and more logically organized version of the British original.

The Israeli legal system cannot be understood in isolation from the fact that, to date, there is no formal constitution. The Declaration of Independence, issued on May 14, 1948 and signed by the members of the National Council, clearly stated that the first permanent elected government would be established under a constitution to be determined by a constituent assembly. Thus, even before the first general election, public opinion was divided over whether the newborn nation was ready for a formal constitution. Opposition was voiced mainly by the orthodox camp due to fears that a constitution would have superior normative status over religious rulings and lead to the separation of state and religion. Objections were also raised by some due to the high priority placed on national security and military needs which, contrary to the principle of equality for all citizens, would inevitably require legislation restricting the freedom of Israel's Arabs.

The public debate regarding the constitution resulted in the adoption of a compromise known as the Harari Resolution. It was agreed that a comprehensive constitution would not be formulated at that stage, but that basic laws delineating important principles would be enacted in a step-by-step process. Indeed, over the years, a series of basic laws have been adopted by the Knesseth (Israeli parliament). A formal constitution has yet to see the light of day; likewise, a bill of rights.

Although many of the basic laws enacted over the years (e.g., the basic law of the Knesseth, the government, the judiciary, the armed forces) represent an important contribution to the constitutional process in Israel, none of them have been ascribed superior normative status over ordinary laws enacted by the Knesseth. In practical terms, this created a situation whereby the Israeli legislature can enact any kind of law, even change a basic law, by majority vote.

The fact that civil and human rights are not protected constitutionally has not meant that such rights have been constantly breached or that due process has been withheld. In a series of landmark cases, the Israel Supreme Court has made it clear that even though civil rights and equality as a legal principle are not anchored in a formal constitution (as in the American system), they are important and significant features in the Israeli legal system.[2] In *Yafora Ltd. v. Israel Broadcasting Authority*,[3] it was made clear that: "It is the law (although at present unwritten) that any discrimination on the grounds of race, sex, belief, political, or other opinion . . . is forbidden for everybody acting under the law." A similar statement was made by the attorney general in *Peretz v. Kfar Shmaryahu*[4] who declared that: "Equality before the law is a basic principle of Israel's legal system. . . . [This principle] has grown to become a well-rooted, binding legal rule." Although these cases do not deal directly with the issue of discrimination, no doubts are left that the principles guiding these two judicial decisions apply to discrimination on the basis of race and national origin.

In March 1992 the Israeli parliament took a major step forward by adopting two important basic laws; namely, Basic Law: Freedom of Occupation and Basic Law: Human Freedom and Dignity. The Basic Law: Freedom of Occupation deals with the right of each and every citizen or resident of the state of Israel to pursue his/her occupation or profession. This basic law was granted superior normative status and can be invalidated only by another basic law ratified by a parliamentary majority. With regard to the Basic Law: Human Freedom and Dignity, questions have been raised as to whether it does indeed cover the full range of human rights. In his article, "Protected Human Rights: Range and Limits" (1993), Supreme Court Judge Aharon Barak provides an interpretation of the intention of the Israeli legislator in enacting this new basic law. According to him, it protects some of the rights that derive from human dignity and freedom, such as the right to own property, the right of liberty, and the right to privacy, but it does not cover the full range of human rights, including the more fundamental right to equality and freedom of speech. In his analysis, Judge Barak points out that the rights which have been left out are contained in the draft of another statute, namely, the Basic Law: Human Rights. According to Judge Barak, rather than focus on the intention of those who drafted the Basic Law: Human Dignity and Freedom, one should focus on the intention of the founders of the state of Israel. The principle of "human dignity and freedom" should encompass all of the implications contained in the notion, "Jewish democratic state." Thus, it should include the full range of rights, including equality, freedom of religious worship, and freedom of speech and expression, even if these are not clearly stated in the current version of the statute. What is more, the Basic Law: Human Dignity and Freedom was not granted superior normative status, and can be limited by a regular statute that seems to serve a reasonable purpose and, in general, complies with the norms and values of the state of Israel.

THE CRIMINAL LAW

The criminal code enacted in 1977 broke with British tradition in a number of respects. Criminal activity in Israel is recorded in criminal investigation files opened by the police. Most of such files are opened following citizens' complaints. Initially, based on British procedure, the decision to bring a suspect to court was made following a preliminary inquiry held in a magistrate's court. This procedure required the submission of evidence by the police linking the suspect to the crime. The judge would then decide on whether to indict the suspect or drop charges and close the file due to lack of sufficient evidence. This procedure was found to be overly time-consuming and put a heavy burden on the magistrate's court judges. In 1958, the Israeli parliament adopted an amendment to section 3 of the criminal procedure law, stipulating that the decision to indict would be made by the district prosecutor on the basis of police evidence and public interest. A decision not to indict can be appealed at the level of the state prosecutor, attorney general, or the High Court of Justice. In certain instances, such as cases involving state security, special public sensitivity, or special status of a suspect, a district prosecutor's decision to indict requires the approval of the attorney general. Section 231 of the criminal procedure law provides the attorney general wide discretionary powers, including the decision to postpone criminal proceedings, with no obligation to specify the grounds for such a decision.

The fact that the approval of the attorney general is required in cases of special sensitivity or special (high) status suspects creates an inequality. In her article, "Administrative Discretion in Law Enforcement," Ruth Gabison (1991) draws attention to the fact that the special treatment provision in certain cases, especially in the case of high-status citizens, carries the potential for differential treatment and even discrimination. On the one hand, in order to avoid public criticism, cases that reach the attorney general's office might receive harsher treatment or, on the other hand, they might also receive special consideration and more lenient treatment. Figure 1 illustrates the flow of decision making in the Israeli criminal justice system.

The state of Israel has retained the three-tier court system operated under the British mandate. The Courts Law (Consolidated Version, 1984) regulates the composition, jurisdiction, and procedures of the judicial system. In ascending order, the three levels of the judicial system are, the magistrate's courts (located in most towns); the district courts (located in Jerusalem, Tel-Aviv, Haifa, Beer-Sheva, and Nazareth), and the Supreme Court in Jerusalem, which serves as the highest court of appeal, as Israel's High Court of Justice, and as a court for constitutional matters. All courts deal with both civil and criminal matters, with the jurisdiction of the magistrate's courts limited to minor criminal matters, carrying a maximum sentence of three years of imprisonment and civil matters with claims of up to one million N.I.S. (New Israeli Shekels).

Trials are normally conducted before a single judge and appeals before a bench of three judges, but on the discretion of the court, a trial can be held before a three-judge bench. Appeals from magistrate's courts appear before

Figure 1
The Decision-making Flow Chart of the Israeli Criminal Justice System

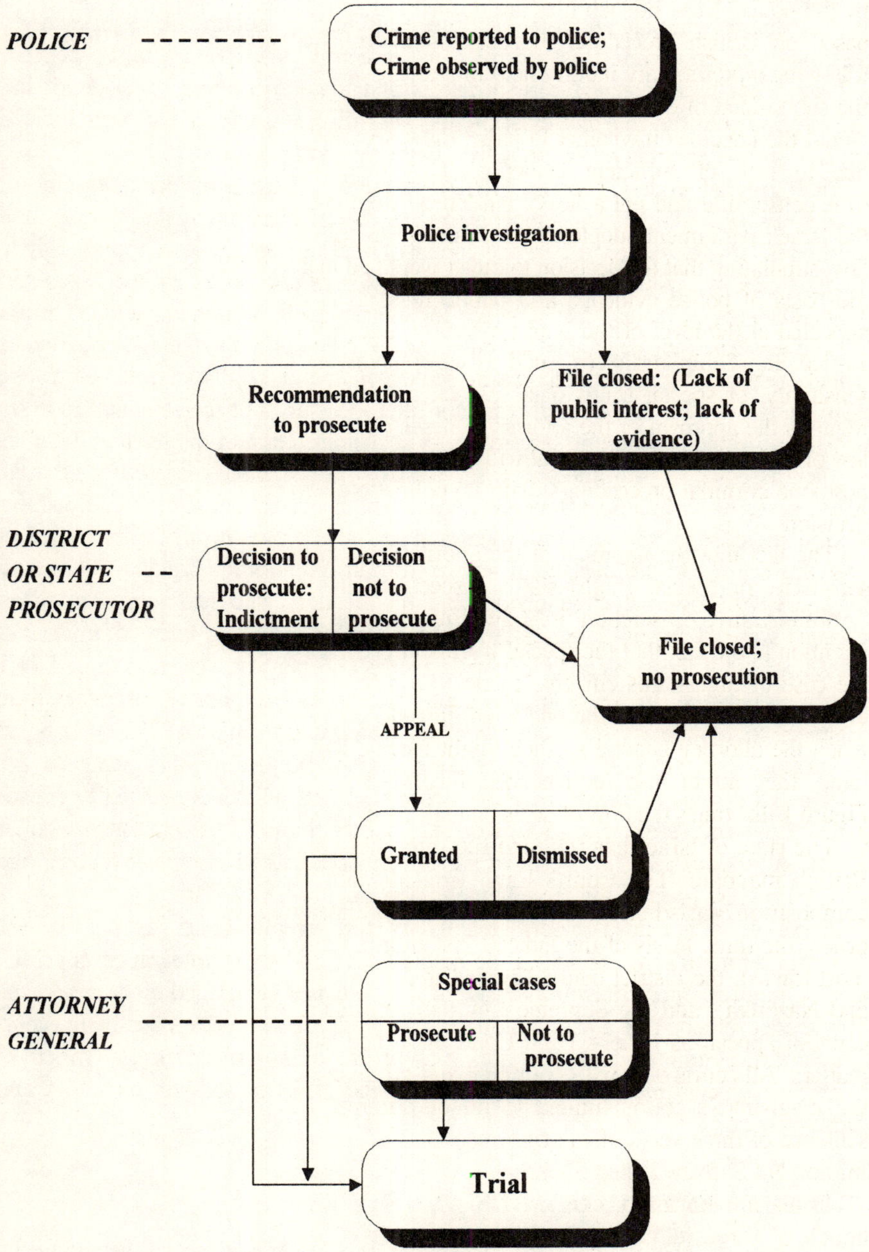

district courts, and appeals from district courts are heard before the Supreme Court. A single appeal is usually considered sufficient, but if not, a district court appeal decision can be challenged in the Supreme Court. Under some circumstances, even the Supreme Court decision may not be the last word; a motion for a rehearing can be filed either by a complainant or by the court itself. Such a motion will be granted if a question of general interest has arisen, if a decision deviates from a rule previously laid down by the Supreme Court, a case is of particular interest, or evidence has become available that did not exist or was not utilized at any of the prior judicial levels. Final judgment is rendered by five Supreme Court judges.

The Criminal Code Ordinance (1936) prescribed a mandatory death penalty for murder. In 1950, Israeli legislation abolished capital punishment for murder and replaced it with mandatory life imprisonment. The death penalty now applies only to offenses such as treason during wartime and offenses committed by the Nazis and their collaborators. Today, life sentence for murder is no longer mandatory, and a reduced sentence may be handed down, at the discretion of the judge. Other penalties include fining, the suspended prison sentence, and a relatively new corrective measure, "service work." According to this latter measure, a prison sentence up to six months can be commuted to "service work" at the discretion of the judge. Offenders are then assigned to full-time public service jobs (in hospitals, community services, etc.), monitored by an officer from the Department of Corrections. However, this form of legal response is still very infrequent and not widely used by all courts. A recent study evaluating the effectiveness of service work in Israel (Nirel, Landau, Sebba, and Sagiv, 1997) showed that recidivism among offenders who had served a prison sentence was 2.4 times higher than among offenders who had been committed to service work. Of those assigned to service work, 71.6 percent were Jewish and 24.1 percent were Arab. In 1993, approximately two thousand criminal offenders were sentenced to community service at about six hundred work places. The widespread assumption that most of the convicted offenders "enjoying" this sentence are white-collar criminals was found to be incorrect. Of all offenders referred to service work, 43 percent were convicted for white-collar crimes and 57 percent for blue-collar crimes. Approximately 75 percent of all service workers had prior convictions, and about 20 percent had already served time in prison.

Probation is practiced widely, mainly by the juvenile court, as part of the rehabilitative approach. For adults, the rehabilitative and social integration approach is most frequently prescribed in the case of drug offenses committed by drug addicts. An offender sentenced to a prison term for a drug offense may be referred by the court to a close institution for treatment during all or part of the prison term. A variety of rehabilitative penal measures are available instead of, or in addition to, fining and imprisonment.

CRIME IN THE LAND OF MILK AND HONEY

In a country characterized by widespread population and social heterogeneity along with deeply rooted alienation and hostility between social factions, one would expect to find high crime rates. However, although much attention has been devoted to almost every aspect of Israel as a heterogeneous society torn by social conflicts, crime has never been considered a major social problem, nor has it featured prominently among the burning issues on the public agenda. On the whole, research into criminal justice disparities has focused mainly on the ethnic dimension within the Jewish population (i.e., Ashkenazi versus Sephardi) rather than the Jewish/Arab dimension. In the following, we describe crime trends in Israel from 1948 to the present. Special attention is paid to differential crime rates among Jews and non-Jews whenever this information was available.

One of the earliest sources of information on the differential involvement of Jews and non-Jews is provided by the two volumes of criminal statistics compiled by Schmeltz and Salzman (1964). This compilation contains crime statistics from the time of the British mandate up to 1962. No other source since then has provided official crime statistics giving the breakdown between Jews and non-Jews or between the various ethnic groups within the Jewish community in Israel.[5] The criminal statistics published annually by the Central Bureau of Statistics as well as in the Israel National Police Annual Report include aggregated data on the distribution of crime among Jews and non-Jews only in rare specific instances. Moreover, criminological research into the treatment of Jews and non-Jews by the Israeli criminal justice system has been based, for the most part, on rather small cross-sectional samples focusing on limited areas of the topic (Schmeltz and Salzman 1962; Reifen 1966; Schmeltz and Salzman 1969; Cohen 1981; Palmor 1982; Frishtik 1983; Cohen 1985; Cohen and Palmor 1985; Hassin 1987; Hassin and Kremnitzer 1988; Cohen 1989).

Since 1948 there has been a continuous rise in the overall number of criminal offenses recorded annually by the Israeli police. The total number increased from 36,700 in 1951 to 61,700 in 1960, and 70,400 in 1962. However, given the dramatic increase in the country's population during this period, the increase in terms of rates per one thousand population since 1951 can be shown to be infinitesimal: in 1951–1952, there were approximately twenty-eight offenses; in 1953–1959, twenty-five to twenty-six offenses; and in 1962, almost thirty offenses per one thousand (Schmeltz and Salzman 1964). These trends are depicted in figure 2.

Figure 3 indicates that during the period of the British mandate as well as during the early years of the state of Israel, the conviction rates were much higher in the Arab sector than in the Jewish sector. The average conviction rate per one thousand in the Jewish population during this period was seven cases, compared to 16.2 cases among the Arabs. This disparity is probably even greater in view of the fact that it does not reflect the higher involvement of Arabs in security offenses (offenses against the Defense [Emergency] Regulations 1945), which are not included in the statistics.

During 1960–1965, there was a 32 percent increase in criminal files opened by the police: 2,611 per one hundred thousand population in 1960, to 3,462 in 1965 (Criminal Statistics, 1974). A variety of events influenced Israeli society in the 1960s. (Note that now we look at a rate per 100,000.)

The period between 1965 and June 1967 was marked by a deep economic recession coupled with high rates of unemployment. Although all levels of Israeli society were hit, the impact was felt especially in the households of lower socioeconomic status families located in development towns. As a consequence, for the first time in its short history, Israel experienced a massive wave of emigration (mainly to North America and Europe) termed "Yerida" (Hebrew word for *descent*).[6]

Figure 2
Trends in the General Crime Index, 1950–1962 (Offenses per 1,000 Population)

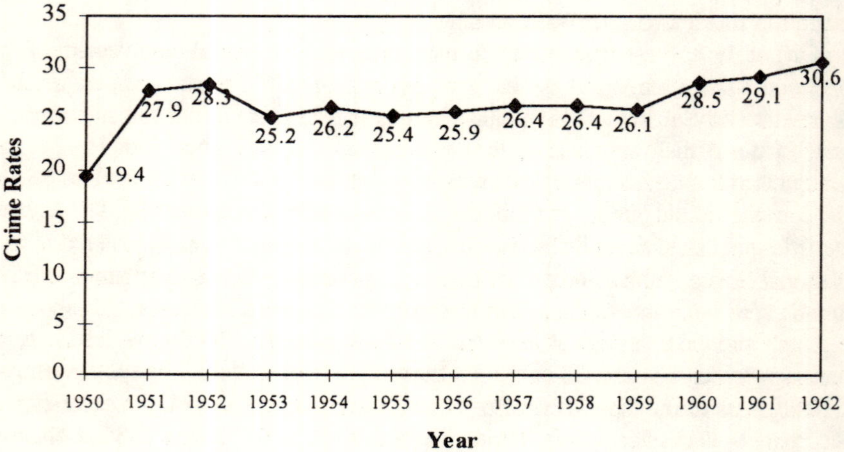

Figure 3
Conviction Rates of Jews and Arabs, 1940–1960 (per 1,000 Population)

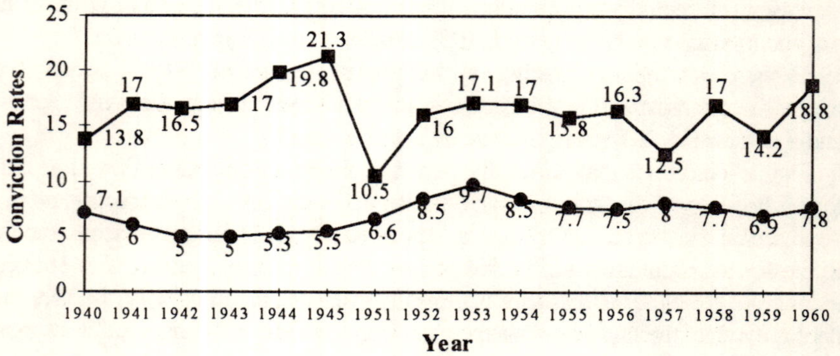

The economic recession ended with the Six-Day War. In June 1967, Israel was simultaneously engaged in war on three fronts with its Arab neighbors—Egypt, Syria, and Jordan. Although the war was one of the shortest on record, its effects were profound. In the course of six days, the Israeli Defense Forces (IDF) captured territories from Syria, Egypt and Jordan.[7] In a study comparing the impact of the 1967 Six-Day War and the 1973 Yom Kippur War on crime trends, Fishman (1983) found that during the wars, the durations of which were very clearly delineated, the crime rates shrunk dramatically, and following the end of belligerence, the rates surged. However, the types of crime that prevailed and increased were different after each of these wars. It seems that the unique characteristics of each war and the economic conditions that followed serve to explain the differential crime increases.

Following the 1967 war, which took a relatively light toll in human lives but inflicted tremendous damage to property, there was a dramatic increase in property crime, including armed robbery (a property offense in the Israeli crime statistics). This increase in property crime can also be attributed to the economic boom that swept the country following the expansion of Israel's sphere of influence, with new economic opportunities attracting investment and development on an unprecedented scale (Fishman and Argov, 1980). After the 1973 Yom Kippur War, with its high death toll and thousands of casualties, there was a dramatic increase in homicide and other crimes of violence in addition to property offenses due to the postwar period of economic hardship. Indeed, the term "national earthquake" aptly described the impact of the 1973 Yom Kippur War. Crime rates (which had increased from 49.3 offenses per one thousand in 1968 to 61.7 in 1972) decreased temporarily to 55.8 offenses per one thousand in 1973 (see figure 4). This shrinking trend can be attributed to short-lived effects of the war: the mobilization of a large part of the male Jewish population between the ages of eighteen and fifty-five for a period of several months, and the sense of general cohesion. However, shortly after the fighting ended, and with the country trying desperately to return to peacetime routine, criminal activity also returned to "normal"—the upward trend that had begun prior to 1973 resumed in 1974, and the crime rates escalated reaching 95.4 per one thousand population in 1980.

Figure 4 shows a brief decline to 82 offenses per one thousand in 1982, which can be attributed in part to the "Peace for the Galilee Operation," a massive IDF attack designed to hit the terrorist infrastructure in southern Lebanon following continuous attempts to disrupt civilian life in the northern region of Israel. This was followed by a gradual increase reaching 87.5 in 1983 and 90.1 in 1985. There was a downward trend in the second half of the 1980s, ending with 78.8 offenses per one thousand population in 1990. Yet another upward turn occurred in the early 1990s, reaching 86.3 per thousand in 1992. Between 1991 and 1992 alone, the increase in the number of files opened by the police was 16 percent. Part of the increase during this period was due to a significant increase in state security offenses, as well as causing bodily harm, arson, and other offenses which may have been related, directly or indirectly, to the Intifada (Palestinian uprising) in the West Bank and parallel unrest among Israeli Arabs. Note that the statistics reported here refer only to offenses committed within the "Green Line" borders of Israel.[8] The overall increase in files opened by the police between 1985 and 1992 was 26 percent, and the increase between 1990 and 1992 was 22 percent. Most of the new files in this latter period were for property offenses

(78%), although a major increase was also observed in files opened for drug offenses (30%).

The general upward trend and the fluctuations observed over the years, as well as the general volume of crime, are not paralleled by the trends recorded for violent crime in general, or homicide and attempted homicide, in particular. In the case of homicide, for example, only very slight changes are discernible, with rates per 100,000 increasing from 1.2 in 1960 to: 1.5 in 1970, 2.0 in 1980, 1.9 in 1990, and 2.2 in 1996.

Figure 4
Police Investigation Files for Selected Years 1960–1992 (Rates per 1,000)

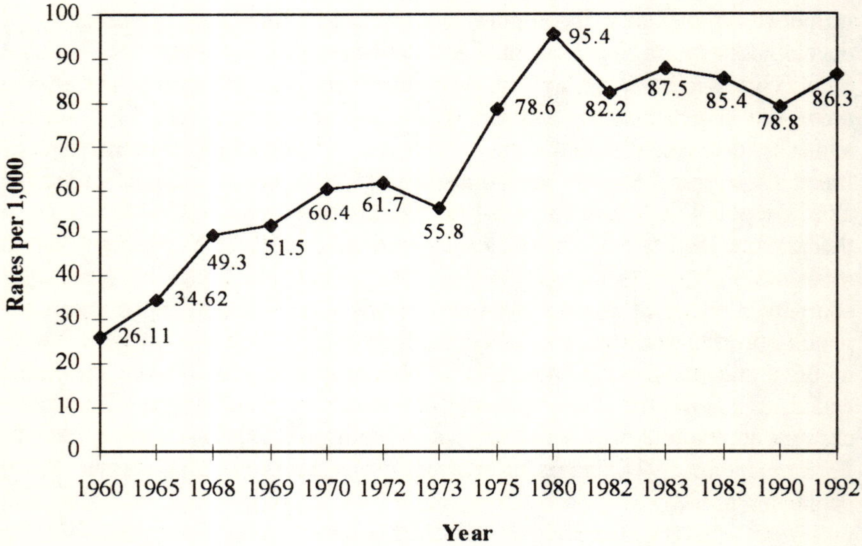

The rates of criminal violence have been so low that it would seem more appropriate to attempt to explain the low rates of violence that have been characteristic in Israeli society rather than dwell on fluctuations and increases. Perhaps the best place to start any such explanation is to realize that Israeli society, rather than representing a revolutionary society, should be viewed as a continuation of the Jewish communities in the Diaspora during the last century. The current low rates of violence and, in particular, the low rates in the first two decades of the country's existence, can be understood in light of the Jewish values and survival mechanisms that kept those communities alive right up to the Holocaust in Europe. The fact that Jews were a minority, often suffering discrimination and persecution, created a need for unity and social cohesion in order to preserve the communal structure so essential to maintaining Jewish life and tradition. The Jews, so often victims of brutality and harassment, developed a moral ideology which despised force, and treated the bully and the thug with the utmost of contempt. Jewish culture promoted spirituality as a way to come to terms with poverty, and idealized "brain power" as opposed to "physical force." It was important to maintain a low profile and not draw too much attention to themselves for fear of retribution on the slightest pretext by the "enemies" around them. To this end, internal social control was developed, and the notion of mutual responsibility was inculcated from an early age. This created a social community virtually free of violence. The establishment of Israel as an independent state produced a very interesting polarity in the attitude towards the place of violence in the emerging social culture. Participation in large-scale violence in the form of national self-defense became an ultimate moral dictate. Military service and fighting in Israel's wars has been a fundamental duty of each and every citizen—a "rite de passage." On the other hand, individual interpersonal violence is still considered a sign of weakness, lack of intelligence, and unbecoming of a civilized person.

Yet another insight into the nonviolent nature of Israeli society is provided by the disassociation between the availability of weapons and the homicide rate. Firearms are readily available to virtually almost all Jewish young men (at the age considered to be the most dangerous in terms of violence). Israeli soldiers are required to carry their weapons not only while on active duty, but also as long as they are in uniform, to and from their army bases. It is therefore amazing that these guns are hardly ever used for criminal purposes. One might wonder whether it ever occurs to young soldiers trying to hitch hike, waiting for hours in the burning sun for someone to stop and pick them up, to use the weapon to hijack a car! Probably not; such behavior would appear to be completely outside the range of the Israeli male's cognitive map.

Be that as it may, cultural intolerance towards violence has never been generalized to include conflicts with the outside world. The sense of being a nation under siege and the trauma of the Holocaust have made the Israelis fanatical about the development of military strength and readiness to resort to force to secure national survival. Indeed, Israelis (especially young men) are heavily involved in violence and violent acts during their military service, in their training as well as in active operations, including wars. It therefore might appear somewhat surprising that the spillover of violence from this domain to the domestic front is so minimal. Again, perhaps an illustration might be appropriate here. During the Palestinian Intifada, the Israeli army exercised authorized force against the Palestinians. They refrained from shooting live bullets however their use of night sticks and tear gas, as well as shooting rubber bullets resulted in many injuries and sometimes even loss of life. The exposure to violence and counter violence was disturbing to one and all. People were concerned as to the effect that such experiences might have on young men—psychological and moral. However, close examination of rates of violence clearly showed that the violent behavior was confined to the military arena, defined by the soldiers as "war action" and, as such, totally divorced from peace time norms of conduct prevailing on the domestic front and in relation to civilian life and relationships.

The low rate of criminal violence is not matched by low crime rates in general. The rates of property crimes, especially burglary, are similar to those observed in most industrialized countries, with a wide gap between high and low income groups.

Examination of the period covered by this study (1980–1992) reveals a seesaw effect: there was an increase in both criminal charges and convictions for serious criminal offenses between 1981 and 1986. This trend was followed by a 20 percent decrease between 1986 and 1988. These rates remained fairly stable until 1990, thereafter followed by a 23 percent increase between 1990 and 1992. The criminal statistics for 1981–1992 indicate that fining was more frequent among non-Jews (61%) than Jews (43%). In 1992, suspended prison sentences were more frequently served on Jews (72%) than non-Jews (68%), and prison terms were imposed more frequently on Jews (26%) than non-Jews (20%). Prison terms were imposed more frequently on recidivists, Jewish and non-Jewish, than on first offenders.

TRENDS IN PENAL POLICY

To date, there has been no attempt to link Israeli crime trends with penal policy on the basis of the outputs of the criminal justice system. However, it is evident from the longitudinal statistics that the continuous gradual upward crime trend over the years has been paralleled by an increasingly punitive approach on the part of the courts. Perusal of the criminal sanctions applied by the courts reveals an increase in the frequency of suspended and actual prison sentences. In 1981, suspended sentences were served on 47 percent of all convicted offenders, in comparison to 56 percent in 1985 and 67 percent in 1992. Actual prison sentences were served on 13.9 percent of all convicted offenders, increasing to 18 percent in 1992. According to the 1992 crime statistics, prison sentences are most frequently handed down for offenses against human life (62.3%) followed by, in descending order, security offenses (32.5%), sex offenses (31.2%), property offenses (21.7%), and assault (8.9%).

The seesaw effect is also evident in the differential treatment of Arabs and Jews. Overall crime rates were higher among Israeli Arabs than among Jews until 1967. Following the abolition of military rule in 1968, the Arab crime rate became temporarily lower than that of Jews, only to be followed by an upward trend in the 1978–1988 period. The Arab population grew from about 11 percent of the total population of Israel in 1964 to approximately 18 percent in the late 1980s, but their contribution to crime increased from 14 percent in 1964 to 18 percent in 1975, reaching 25 percent in 1988.

Although it is tempting to attribute the overrepresentation of Arabs in the criminal statistics to direct discrimination, it seems that more careful analysis is in order because this period also includes decreases in their crime rates and no one would interpret these as reflecting increased tolerance towards the Arab minority. One explanation for the high crime rate among Arabs during military rule is the more intensive scrutiny to which they were subjected during that period. The decline in the crime rates followed soon after the abolition of military rule, which for the first time since the establishment of Israel, allowed freedom of movement for Arabs; hence, their lesser visibility (not necessarily lower crime rates). The increase in Arab crime rates over the past twenty years also reflects the general socioeconomic position of the Arab population as a group. Their higher per capita involvement in antisocial acts must surely be attributed, apart from anything else, to the fact that, on average, they are less educated and poorer than their Jewish counterparts. The question whether Arabs are discriminated against in the Israeli criminal justice system can only be answered if we control for variables, such as offense type and previous criminal history, as well as socio demographic characteristics like age and gender. However, the answer to the more general question of whether Arabs are subject to discrimination, and whether the fact that more crime is committed by them is testimony to such discrimination, must surely be in the positive. Such discrimination is evident in the opportunity structure, the budgetary allocation to Arab municipalities for education, social welfare services, and the like. Poverty does not breed itself: it results from societal priorities regarding where to invest limited resources. A decision to prefer one sector over another has consequences, not only as far as poverty is concerned, but also regarding the breeding ground of crime.

NOTES

1. *Bourkan v. Minister of Finance* (1978) 32 P.D. II 800,81,83,86 (nn11,13),88(n25), 128.

2. *Kol Ha'am v. Minister of Interior* (1953) 7 P.D. 871. In: David, Kretzmer *The Legal Status of Arabs in Israel,* Westview Special Studies on the Middle East, 1990.

3. Yafora Ltd. v. Broadcasting Authority (1971) 25 P.D. II 741. In: Kretzmer, David, *The Legal Status of Arabs in Israel,* Westview Special Studies on the Middle East, 1990.

4. *Peretz v. Kfar Shmaryahu Local Council* (1962)16 P.D. 2101.

5. Crime statistics retained within the Israeli police computerized archives contain an indication as to nationality. However, this information is not usually released in the annual crime statistics published by the police or the Central Bureau of Statistics. Since 1982 there has been no breakdown by Jewish ethnic groups.

6. "Yerida" has a negative connotation in that it is applied to people who prove themselves incapable of sustaining the stress and difficulties of life in Israel and therefore decide to leave for an easier life in another country.

7. The effect of the occupation and contribution of the Palestinian population living in the occupied territories on crime in Israel will be discussed in chapter 6.

8. The "Green Line" refers to the borders of Israel prior to the 1967 Six-Day War; hence, the crime statistics presented here do not include offenses committed in the West Bank and Gaza Strip territories.

2

Racial and Ethnic Injustice

THEORETICAL PERSPECTIVES

We know very little about ethnic injustice in ancient times. However, in the modern era, attention has been called to disparities and inequities at every stage of the criminal justice process, from arrest to final disposition. Judging by the number of studies on the subject, it seems that special attention has been devoted to disparities in sentencing—racial, ethnic, national, gender and age (Bullock 1961; Hagan 1974; Hagan and Albonetti 1982; Johnson 1941; Kleck 1981; Petersilia 1983; Spohn et al. 1981-1982; Zatz, 1984). To date, most of such studies have focused on the United States, with little attention devoted to other societies. In view of its wide ethnic, national, and social diversity, it would seem that Israel provides an ideal setting for the study of disparities within its criminal justice system. This study will focus on how Arabs fare in the system in comparison to Jews. We analyze on the one hand the effect of legal and extralegal variables on three crucial junctures in the judicial process; namely, police closure of criminal files, conviction, and sentencing. On the other hand we examine also how both Jews and Arabs themselves perceive the criminal justice system in its functioning and relate to it via their attitudes.

The existing body of research into disparities in the criminal justice system is probably best summarized by Zatz (1984), who stated that "the sum of our knowledge is that for some offenses, in some jurisdictions, controlling for some legal and extralegal factors, at some historical points, and using some methodologies, some groups are differentially treated." The findings in this research area have been inconclusive. However, this has not prevented continued investigation of the subject and important issues related to it—on the contrary.

Several major studies have dealt with the issue of racial and ethnic discrimination in the criminal justice system. Petersilia (1983) examined racial discrimination in California, Michigan, and Texas based on a survey of 1,380 male inmates in the three states. The findings clearly showed that Hispanic and African American defendants received heavier sentences than white defendants with similar criminal histories who were convicted for comparable felonies.

Many of the studies conducted in the 1980s failed to find significant ethnic or racial disparities in the various levels of the judicial process; the few disparities that were found in post arrest case processing were relatively minor and tended to be balanced by disparities in other decisions along the way (Blumstein 1982; Hagan and Peterson 1984; Klein et al. 1990; Kleck 1981; Myers and Talerico 1987; Petersilia, 1983; Spohn et al. 1981-82). In contrast, Nelson's (1994) study, which analyzed disparities in post arrest case processing while controlling for differences in arrest, charge, and prior criminal record, found that from 1985 through 1986, minorities were incarcerated more frequently than whites in the state of New York. Disparities were least likely to occur in "no prior arrest" cases and arrests for "misdemeanor crimes." Defendants with a record of prior arrests and those arrested for misdemeanor crimes with prior arrests were about as likely to be affected by disparities as those arrested for felony crimes. Another study (Farnworth et al. 1991) found dramatic contrasts between the processing of Hispanic and white male defendants with a prior record: white males were far more likely to have their primary charges reduced to misdemeanors and to receive probation, while Hispanic males, in contrast, were twice as likely to be sentenced to prison. Labeling theory has provided explanations as to why members of the Hispanic minority group are exposed to more severe sentencing. A study conducted by Zatz (1984), which included whites, African Americans, and Chicanos, found that prior criminal record affected severity of punishment, especially in the case of Chicanos. The effect of prior criminal record was explained in terms of negative perceptions of Chicano narcotic violators who were described as "insidious" and "subversive." A recent study (Holmes et al. 1996) found that it is not only the legal background of Hispanics that influences legal decision making, but also the defendants' access to legal resources and representation by private counsel. This study focused on the role of ethnicity and employment in the felony adjudication process in two southwestern jurisdictions. These status variables were found to have an effect on the likelihood of obtaining private representation and release on bail, two factors that subsequently influence sentencing. Ethnicity also directly influenced sentence severity in one jurisdiction: defendants who were members of ethnic minorities or who were unemployed were found to be disadvantaged in the adjudication process.

Farnworth et al. hypothesized that Hispanics, more than African Americans, lacked the social and personal resources needed to resist the deviant label (prior criminal record, etc.) imposed by court sanctions. Their socioeconomic standing in society, stereotyping, and their language difficulties hampered their negotiation in the criminal justice system. The author concludes that these findings are consistent with expectations derived from the tenets of labeling. Although no measures of ethnic stereotypes were employed in this study, the findings are indicative of the use of repressive social control against "a fast-growing minority group that threatens the established power structure in our society" (Farnworth et al. 1991). The study also pointed out the important role played by factors such as prior criminal record, and possible links to stereotypes and the social status of minority group members. However, even efforts to correct unwarranted sentencing disparity via reforms, such as sentencing guidelines, have failed to remedy the problem. In a recent study, Kramer and Ulmer (1996) focused on the degree to which sentences that depart from state guidelines involved extralegal variables. Their findings suggest that although legally prescribed factors such as offense type/severity and criminal history are the primary predictors of judicial decisions, extralegal factors such as race and gender also play an important role.

The theoretical framework of a study conducted by Dixon (1995) explains specific outcomes of criminal sentencing using a three-pronged approach. The first, the *substantive political perspective*, views criminal processing as a politically organized process in which social class and status affect the outcome. The second, the *formal legal perspective*, accepts the Weberian notion that the organization of justice is based on technical rationality and is guided strictly by formal rules. The third, the *organizational maintenance approach*, views sentencing as a process created by courtroom elites who come to share common interests in disposing of cases. The substantive political perspective would seem to be strongly guided by conflict theory, theory which clearly addresses issues pertinent to racial inequality, in general, and disparities in the criminal justice system, in particular (Marx 1859; Bonger 1969; Dahrendorf 1959). The operative assumptions of this approach are that power, and political power in particular, is distributed unequally and, therefore, formal social control is distributed unequally as well. The formal legal perspective contends that formal legal rules govern sentencing decisions via the application of the rules to the specific case. The assumption here is that sentencing outcomes are mainly the result of legal rules and criteria applied equally to defendants of all classes, races and ethnic groups (Lukacs 1971); hence, legal factors are the major determinants of sentencing outcomes. According to the organizational maintenance approach, sentencing is perceived as an organizational process maintained by courtroom elites. Due in part to the complexity of the tasks required of such courtroom elites, there is a shared common interest, the main goal being efficient disposal of cases. The goal of maintaining a stable and efficient system is achieved by developing tools such as "presumption of innocence" and "plea bargaining." According to this perspective, social characteristics such as class and race have no significant effect on sentencing outcomes.

In general, the research findings on racial and ethnic disparities are inconclusive. The findings of earlier studies tend to be supportive of the claim that African Americans are disadvantaged relative to white defendants (Lynch and Groves 1989; Petersilia 1983). However, the findings of these studies have been contested on methodological grounds, such as failure to control for criminal history or type of offense (Hagan 1974; Zatz 1984). In an attempt to reconcile conflicting findings, Zatz suggested that although overt racial discrimination may not exist in the court processing of criminals, more subtle discrimination is likely to be disclosed through the use of various models and interaction variables which present the findings in a more cumulative mode.

The inconsistent findings on discrimination and sentencing disparities demonstrate the need for a contextual analysis of sentencing processes; an analysis that would take into account the social and political environment in which the criminal justice system operates (Hagan and Bumiller 1983; Myers and Talerico 1987).

NATIONALITY AND INJUSTICE IN ISRAEL

That disparities exist in the criminal justice system in Israel, especially between Jews and Arabs, is assumed by many and disputed by some. It is therefore somewhat surprising that this issue has not been investigated exhaustively. The findings that are available are based on a series of rather small-scale studies conducted over the years. For instance, a study of probation decisions (Cohen and Palmor 1985) found that probation was granted proportionately more often to Jewish (44.8%) than to Arab (17.5%) adult offenders even when there was control for severity of the current offense. Another study (Fishman and Soroka 1980) comparing the disposition of Arab and Jewish cases in the district courts of Haifa and Nazareth found that prison sentences were served more frequently on Arab offenders (53.1%) than on Jews (27.7%), and that Jewish offenders were given suspended prison sentences more often (44.6%) than Arab offenders (37.5%). Moreover, only 9.4 percent of the Arab offenders were given probation, in comparison to 27.7 percent of the Jewish offenders. However, a third study (Cohen 1985) based on 162 adult males sentenced in two district courts, found the relationship between sentencing and nationality to be spurious. Although the likelihood of Arab offenders to receive prison terms was nearly twice as high as that of Jewish offenders, it was found that this disparity was a function of the severity of the offense; that is, Arab offenders were sentenced to prison terms more often than Jews for committing more serious offenses, and not because they were Arabs.

A larger-scale study conducted by Frishtik (1983), based on a sample of 1,194 adults sentenced between 1978 and 1981, revealed that even after controlling for type of offense, Arab offenders were more likely to receive prison sentences (62%) than Jewish offenders (48%). Hassin and Kremnitzer (1988), pursuing the same line of investigation under more controlled conditions, examined the sentencing outcomes of Jewish and Arab traffic violators. The findings in this study showed that the more severe sanctions, such as license confiscation, were much more likely to be imposed on Arabs (61.9%) than on Jews (24.1%). However, it appears that this large overall discrepancy was largely influenced by the heavy sentences imposed on both Jews and Arabs by one judge in one courtroom, where the bulk of the defendants were Arabs.

In a 1989 report entitled *Crime, Justice, and Social Control in the Israeli-Arab Population*, Stanley Cohen examined 52,832 files of Jews and

Arabs processed through the criminal justice system in 1987. Cohen's main hypothesis was that because the courts in Israel are predominantly "Jewish institutions," they treat the Jews and Arabs who appear in them differently. Much of Cohen's empirical evidence seems to be in support of this hypothesis. Two major categories of decisions were studied: file closure due to "lack of evidence" and "lack of public interest." Of the files closed due to "lack of public interest," 46 percent pertained to Jewish suspects, compared to only 29 percent pertaining to Arab suspects. In addition, the likelihood of unwarranted arrest was higher among Arab juveniles than among Jewish juveniles. However, with regard to the average number of convictions, only slightly more Arabs (80.6%) than Jews (74.6%) had one to five convictions per offender, and more Jewish offenders than Arabs had six to twelve previous convictions. The mean number of convictions per adult Jewish offender was 4.4, compared to 3.8 for adult Arab offenders. Prison sentences for terms longer than three years were found for 15.1 percent of the convicted Arabs, compared to 12.9 percent of the Jews. Thus, Cohen's detailed findings on the differential and systematically discriminatory treatment of Arabs in the Israeli criminal justice system are far from conclusive. In Cohen's own words, a "more sophisticated" analysis is called for, one that will be based on a more representative sample, controlling for variables such as type of offense, recidivism, and other background indicators.

A more methodologically elaborate study (Rattner 1996) recently examined the effect of legal and extralegal variables on prison sentencing. Based on a sample of eight thousand criminal files for the years 1988–1989, the results indicate that when no variables are controlled for, "being an Israeli Arab" is associated with only a slightly higher probability of being sentenced to prison than "being a Jew." In general, although the probability of receiving a prison sentence is higher the more serious the offense, the probability of Arab offenders receiving a prison sentence is higher than that of Jewish offenders at the same level of offense severity. Similarly, in the case of recidivism, Arab recidivists are more likely to receive a prison sentence than Jewish recidivists: Arab offenders with two prior felony convictions are almost twice as likely to be imprisoned than their Jewish counterparts. This discrepancy was found to be even greater for chronic offenders (three or more prior convictions). However, the discrepancies with regard to imprisonment were not consistent across all offenses. Although there was no significant difference in the handing down of prison sentences on Arabs and Jews convicted for property offenses, the probability of a prison sentence in the case of violent offenses (bodily harm) was much higher for Arabs than Jews. The explanation for the higher likelihood of Arabs being sentenced to prison terms probably lies in the nature of the period in which the sample was selected—the study was based on the analysis of files recorded from 1988–1989, the peak of the Intifada (the Palestinian uprising against Israeli military rule in the West Bank and Gaza Strip). Although this study did not employ any measures of social distance or hostility, it is not implausible to assume that the events which took place in those years resulted in increased tension and heightened social control. Thus, it is possible that increased hostility and social distance between Jews and Arabs was translated into an increased perception of Arab offenders as dangerous; hence, their more severe treatment by the courts. It is too early to say whether these findings represent a temporary response to a specific situation, or whether they reflect a growing social problem which will have serious consequences for the social fabric of Israeli society long after the specific cause ceases to be relevant.

The distribution of sentences by nationality and recidivism presented in table 1 (Israel Central Bureau of Statistics, 1992) shows that, across the board, imprisonment was imposed more frequently on convicted Jewish first offenders (18%) than on Arab first offenders (12.3%). Fines, on the other hand, were imposed, overall, more frequently on Arab first offenders (58.1%) than on Jewish first offenders (40.2%). A similar pattern is obtained for recidivists—prison sentences were imposed more frequently on Jewish recidivists (25.1%) than on Arab recidivists (19.3%).

The pattern of differential sanctions imposed on convicted offenders becomes more complicated when offense category is taken into account. Arabs found guilty of offenses against the security of the state were treated more severely (sentenced to prison) than Jewish offenders in the same crime category (first offenders: Arabs 41.7%, Jews 18.6%; recidivists: Arabs 40.8%, Jews 23.7%).

Table 1
Distribution of Sentences by Nationality and Recidivism (in percent)

	Adults				**Juveniles**			
	Jews		**Arabs**		**Jews**		**Arabs**	
	First Offenders	**Recidivists**	**First Offenders**	**Recidivists**	**First Offenders**	**Recidivists**	**First Offenders**	**Recidivists**
Total	**7,982**	**17,906**	**3,230**	**7,139**	**1,355**	**911**	**544**	**283**
Percent	100	100	100	100	100	100	100	100
General								
Prison	18.0	25.1	12.3	19.3	0.5	5.2	2.4	12.0
Prison + fine	2.5	2.9	3.2	3.4	-	0.3	0.4	0.4
Fine	40.2	40.2	58.1	57.3	32.2	39.1	43.9	40.3
Other	39.4	31.7	20.1	26.5	67.3	55.4	55.3	47.3
Security								
Total	**86**	**173**	**204**	**238**	**16**	**1**	**24**	**3**
Percent	100	100	100	100	100	100	100	100
Prison	18.6	23.7	41.7	40.8	-	-	-	12.5
Prison + fine	7.0	4.9	20.6	8.8	-	-	-	-
Fine	29.1	58.4	29.9	44.1	31.3	-	29.2	66.7
Other	45.3	13.9	7.8	6.3	68.8	100	58.3	33.3

Table 1 – *Continued*

	Adults				Juveniles			
	Jews		Arabs		Jews		Arabs	
	First Offen-ders	Recid-ivists	First Offen-ders	Recid-ivists	First Offen-ders	Recid-ivists	First Offen-ders	Recid-ivists
Public Order								
Total	**2,615**	**4,912**	**924**	**1,846**	**177**	**210**	**101**	**81**
Percent	100	100	100	100	100	100	100	100
Prison	32	20	8.4	11.1	-	6.7	4	16
Prison + fine	1.6	1.3	1.8	2.0	-	0.5	-	-
Fine	31.4	41.4	56.9	60.3	33.3	31.0	31.7	24.7
Other	35.0	37.3	32.8	26.6	66.7	61.9	64.4	59.3
Against Person's Life								
Total	**67**	**33**	**124**	**50**	**7**	**4**	**19**	**12**
Percent	100	100	100	100	100	100	100	100
Prison	61.2	54.5	76.6	76.0	-	42.9	16.7	-
Prison + fine	6.0	12.1	6.5	16.0	-	-	-	10.5
Fine	17.9	19.1	7.3	4.0	28.6	25.0	31.6	33.3
Other	14.9	24.2	9.7	4.0	28.6	75.0	57.9	50.0
Bodily Harm								
Total	**1,509**	**2,528**	**638**	**1,304**	**224**	**155**	**107**	**42**
Percent	100	100	100	100	100	100	100	100
Prison	5.5	12.8	6.3	9.2	0.4	2.6	4.7	9.5
Prison + fine	0.7	1.4	0.8	2.1	-	-	-	-
Fine	32.6	42.0	55.3	63.1	30.4	40.0	41.1	50.0
Other	61.2	43.8	37.6	25.5	69.2	57.4	54.2	40.5
Property Offense								
Total	**1,381**	**4,504**	**619**	**1,541**	**769**	**453**	**253**	**121**
Percent	100	100	100	100	100	100	100	100
Prison	8.5	33.2	8.9	25.2	0.3	4.2	0.4	9.1
Prison + fine	1.9	2.9	1.5	2.9	-	0.2	-	0.8
Fine	39.5	33.8	59.9	51.7	33.3	42.6	49.4	46.3
Other	50.1	30.1	29.7	20.2	66.4	53.0	50.2	43.8

Source: Criminal Statistics (Central Bureau of Statistics, 1992).

Although our data is presented in terms of crime categories rather than specific offenses, it can still be argued that crime severity plays an important role and we may speculate that due to nationalistic motives, Arabs may have been involved in more serious offenses than Jews. Although the nature of security offenses may have been merely technical, Arabs may have been more seriously involved in actions that are considered serious in terms of loyalty and national identity.

In the case of offenses against public order, Jews seem to be more severely punished (sent to prison) than Arabs (first offenders: Jews 32%, Arabs 8.4%; recidivists: Jews 20%, Arabs 11.1%). Offenders committing serious violent offenses (against human life) are perceived as a greater threat to the public and, therefore, more severe sanctions are to be expected. The threat is perceived as even greater when such offenses are committed by members of minority groups, especially if this group is also perceived as hostile. Statistics for 1992 in the offenses against human life category show that Arabs were sentenced to prison more frequently than Jews (first offenders: Arabs 76.6%, Jews 61.2%; recidivists: Arabs 76.0%, Jews 54.5%). These marked sentencing discrepancies narrow significantly in the category of causing bodily harm—prison sentences were imposed only on 6.3 percent of the Arab and 5.5 percent of the Jewish first offenders, and on 9.2 percent of the Arab and 12.8 percent of the Jewish recidivists. In cases such as these, the circumstances of the crime (which are not specified in the crime statistics employed in the current study) play an important role in determining the severity of punishment. Indeed, caution needs to be exercised in attempting to interpret findings related to court statistics that do not take into consideration the unique circumstances of the offense. This, however, is an inherent limitation of using secondary data.

In a study by Haj Yihieh, Rahav, and Teichman (1994) based on 852 police records of 525 Jews and 326 Arabs for the years 1982–1983, an attempt was made to measure bias in the imposition of criminal sanctions in five municipal courts. The findings of this study clearly show that convicted Jews were treated more leniently than the Arabs convicted for the same offense. Disparities were found both in the type of punishment imposed by the courts, as well as in the length of prison sentences.

The actual involvement of Israeli Arabs in crime and their interaction with the criminal justice system is only one side of the coin. The other pertains to their attitudes to, and perceptions of, the judicial system. A limited number of studies have dealt with this side of the picture. In a study conducted by Zureik (1988), close to two-thirds of Israeli Arabs sampled in the early 1980s classified the Zionist movement as racist. A similar proportion called for the repeal of the Law of Return.[1] The results of the same survey administered to Jews at that same point in time are hardly surprising—it was found that 96 percent would welcome the opportunity to see fewer Arabs remain in Israel, and 87 percent indicated that the surveillance of Arabs in Israel should be intensified. Findings of a small case study involving two hundred respondents from two Arab villages regarding their perception of Israeli democracy found that Arabs have less confidence in the courts, the police, and other Israeli institutions. Respondents in the same study also expressed the feeling that when it comes to civil liberties and citizens' rights, they are not protected to the same extent as the Jews (Simon, in Cohen 1989).

The results of three surveys of attitudes among Jews conducted in 1975, 1986, and 1987, reported by Simon and Landis (1990) indicate that 58, 46, and 32 percent, respectively, fully agreed with the statement that there was no discrimination against Arabs in Israel. In a different study (Zureik 1991) results confirmed the expectation that Arabs and Jews diverge in important ways in terms of their perception of the criminal justice system in Israel. Zureik found that Arabs are more critical of police conduct and less inclined to believe that Israeli law guarantees equal treatment for all citizens. According to this study, Arabs also reject the assumption that Israel has no laws discriminating against Arabs. A more complete picture of the extent to which Jews and Arabs diverge in their perceptions of the criminal justice system could have been obtained if additional statistical analyses commonly used in the measurement of perceptions and attitudes were conducted. In yet another study, Rattner (1994) examined the attitudes of Jews and Arabs towards the law and the legal system, as well as perceptions of injustice in the two groups. It was found that there was general support for the legal system and willingness to comply with the law by both Jews and Arabs. However, paradoxically, some 61 percent of the Arab respondents expressed the view that a citizen has to obey only those laws that seem reasonable to him. This apparent inconsistency accommodating legitimization of possible disobedience may well be due to the existence of a deep sense of injustice in the Arab population.

This particular issue will thus become the second scope of our study. Not only are we interested in how the Israeli criminal justice system relates to members of various national groups (Jews, Arabs, and Palestinians), but we attempt to examine how Jews and Arabs relate via their attitudes and perceptions to the law and the criminal justice system. At the same time, we will investigate to what extent feelings of discrimination and injustice contribute to delegitimation of the law, perhaps even to a point where individuals justify violating the law.

Although the findings on the differential processing of Jews and Arabs in the criminal justice system remain equivocal, studies conducted in the past decade provide an abundance of evidence that public stereotypes of Arabs are negative, and may affect law enforcement policy, as well as sentencing outcomes. A study by Fishman, Rattner, and Weimann (1987) examined the impact of ethnicity on the attribution of criminal offenses to faces seen in portrait photos of Jews and Arabs. Apart from fraud (Arabs 20%, Jews 50%), all crimes were more likely to be attributed to portraits of Arabs. Arabs had the highest chance of being associated with the offense of rape (Arabs 49%, Jews 26%), homicide (Arabs 40%, Jews 30%), burglary (Arabs 40%, Jews 25%), and robbery (Arabs 32%, Jews 27%). Similar patterns were obtained in another study (Zureik and Moughrabi 1988). Here, 605 Jewish subjects indicated that the crimes perceived as more likely to be committed by Arabs are security offenses (77%), murder (43%), and rape (33%). The findings of these studies have both theoretical and practical implications. On the theoretical level, they reveal much about the effect of ethnicity on labeling behavior. Ethnic origin, although only implied in a portrait photograph, was the most powerful factor in determining the attribution of offense; it was the major factor in the attribution of crimes, even more powerful than social distance between subjects from different ethnic groups. Furthermore, the stereotypes were so strong that they were also found in members of the ethnic group labeled. Thus, Arabs attributed rape to Arabs at much higher rates than they did to non-Arabs. This supports the cardinal argument of attribution theory; namely, that people have well-established sets of social categories which they use for making decisions and attributions about other people and situations. It also indicates the tremendous power of stereotypes on people.

In the foreword of the book, *Two Volumes of Sentencing* (Golomb, 1992), Judge Haim Cohen, former deputy president of the Israeli Supreme Court, expresses deep concern that Israelis have naively deluded themselves into believing that they have the moral and spiritual strength to fulfill the message delivered in the Declaration of Independence: to grant equality to all inhabitants regardless of race, religion, and gender. The reality, he says is that the Israeli criminal justice system has neglected one of its cornerstone duties—distributing justice to all people. According to Judge Cohen, differential injustice is now rooted in, and an inseparable part of, the process of the imposition of criminal sanctions. The system favors Jews over Arabs.

Thus, two issues will be the focus of our concern in this book. The central one is to establish whether important rulings regarding issues such as legal rights and guilt/innocence are based on social categories like nationality and socioeconomic status and the stereotypes associated with them, or whether decisions of such crucial significance are based mainly on legal factors. Second, we will examine whether the criminal justice system in its functioning has left any imprints in the form of negative attitudes with a sense of injustice and discrimination, that under certain circumstances may justify the notion of "taking the law into one's own hands."

NOTE

1. The Law of Return, 1950, is one of the most important expressions of the Jewish state. Section 1 of the law provides every Jew with the right to come to Israel and to acquire Israeli nationality.

3

Data and Methods

The data for the present study was sampled from the computerized data base of the Israel Police Headquarters. A sample of 3,637 subjects whose first criminal files were opened during 1980–1990 were drawn randomly for each year of this period. First-offense files for 1990 were followed up until December 1992. The actual retrieval of data took place in February 1993. The study focused on serious offenses (i.e., defined as felonies and misdemeanors) committed within the borders of Israel for which a suspect was apprehended.[1] The files include information about the type of offense committed, file closure decisions, and the judicial procedure (trial, conviction, sentencing). The entire criminal history of each sample subject was also retrieved. All personal information, such as name and identity number, was removed from the files by the police. This sampling procedure yielded a data base of 97,001 files.

Most of the files refer to Israeli citizens (Jews and Arabs) apprehended for offenses committed within the borders of the state of Israel. However, owing to the fact that our sampling procedure was completely random, the data base also contained files related to two other subpopulations: (a) Palestinian Arabs living in the West Bank and the Gaza Strip with files for offenses committed within the borders of Israel; and (b) Israeli citizens and Palestinian Arabs residing in the West Bank and Gaza Strip with files for offenses committed in the occupied territories. All files for offenses committed outside the borders of Israel that were not handled by the Israeli criminal justice system were excluded from the analysis. All files opened against Palestinian Arabs who committed crimes within the borders of Israel (5,942 files) are analyzed separately (see chapter 6). Files opened for non-Arab or non-Jews (e.g., non-Arab Christians) were also excluded due to their small number (2.2%). Many of these involved tourists, and the decision to prosecute or not depended on the presence of the person in the country.

DISTRIBUTION OF THE CRIMINAL FILES

Table 2 presents the distribution of the total sample of files by crime category and nationality (including Palestinians from the West Bank and Gaza Strip apprehended for crimes committed within the borders of the state) and Table 3 presents the distribution of the files after the exclusion of files related to Palestinians.

Table 2 shows that the involvement of Palestinian Arabs (from the West Bank and Gaza Strip) in security offenses in Israel is much higher than that of Jews or Israeli Arabs (Palestinians 53.28%, Israeli Arabs 26.4%, Jews 20.3%). This high frequency of files for security offenses among the Palestinians can be attributed to the Intifada (Palestinian uprising) which erupted in December 1987. Although most of the actions taken by Palestinians were confined to the occupied territories, rock-throwing (defined as an offense against human life in the criminal law) did also occur within Israel. Overall, Palestinians accounted for 10.93 percent of the files opened for offenses against human life (rock-throwing, as well as homicide, attempted homicide, and manslaughter), in comparison to Israeli Arabs (57.65%) and Jews (31.42%). However, the low proportion of Palestinian files in this category may reflect a lower clearance rate, rather than lesser criminal involvement. A more detailed analysis of Palestinian criminal involvement is given in chapter 6.

METHOD

The first step in the analysis of data was to examine the distribution of the main independent variables; namely, nationality, type of offense, and gender. Next, we moved to the multivariate stage using a logistic regression analysis in order to examine the likelihood of the occurrence of an event (file closure, conviction, etc.). Logistic regression analysis has been found useful in predicting whether an event will or will not occur, and in identifying the main variables contributing to the prediction. Thus, logistic regression is a mathematical modeling approach that can be used to describe the relationship of several independent variables to a dichotomous dependent variable. Other modeling approaches are possible also, but logistic regression is by far the most appropriate modeling procedure used to analyze event data when the event measure is dichotomous. Because logistic regression models are nonlinear, an iterative algorithm is necessary for parameter estimation. In order to facilitate interpretation of the logistic coefficients, the equations were rewritten in terms of the estimated probability of an event occurring. The logistic function which describes the mathematical form on which the logistic model is based is as follows:

$$f(z) = \frac{1}{1 + e^{-z}} \qquad (1)$$

Table 2
Distribution of Police Files by Crime Category and Nationality

Crime Category	Jews	Arabs	Palestinians	Total
Security	**335**	**435**	**878**	**1,648**
	20.32[1]	26.40	53.28	2.50
	0.71[2]	*3.36*	*14.78*	
Public Order	**10,560**	**3,116**	**733**	**14,409**
	73.29	21.63	5.09	21.85
	22.43	*24.07*	*12.34*	
Offenses Against Persons	**115**	**211**	**40**	**366**
	31.42	57.65	10.93	0.55
	0.24	*1.63*	*0.67*	
Offenses Against Body	**6,545**	**2,040**	**412**	**8,997**
	72.75	22.67	4.58	13.64
	13.90	*15.76*	*6.93*	
Sex Offenses	**655**	**148**	**114**	**910**
	71.98	16.26	11.76	1.38
	1.39	*1.14*	*1.80*	
Vice Offenses	**3,918**	**722**	**439**	**5,079**
	77.14	14.22	8.64	7.70
	8.32	*5.58*	*7.39*	
Property Offenses	**18,617**	**5,328**	**2,538**	**26,483**
	70.30	20.12	9.58	40.15
	39.55	*41.15*	*42.71*	
Fraud Offenses	**4,914**	**706**	**237**	**5,857**
	83.90	12.05	4.05	8.88
	10.44	*5.45*	*3.99*	
Economic Offenses	**700**	**96**	**72**	**868**
	80.65	11.06	8.29	1.32
	1.49	*0.74*	*1.21*	
Administrative Offenses	**45**	**52**	**436**	**533**
	8.44	9.76	81.80	0.81
	0.10	*0.40*	*7.34*	
Licensing Offenses	**343**	**47**	**20**	**410**
	83.66	11.46	4.88	0.62
	0.73	*0.36*	*0.34*	
Other	**324**	**46**	**30**	**400**
	81.00	11.50	7.50	0.61
	0.69	*0.36*	*0.50*	
Total	**47,071**	**12,947**	**5,942**	**65,960**
	71.36	19.63	9.01	100.0

1. Row percentage
2. Column percentage

The values of z are from $-\infty$ to $+\infty$. When z is $-\infty$ the logistic function equals 0 and when z is $+\infty$ then the logistic function equals 1. The logistic function can be interpreted in terms of the probability of an event to occur or not, and can be written as follows:

$$Z = B_0 + B_1X_1 + B_2X_2 + \ldots B_pX_p \quad (2)$$

At each decision stage in the criminal procedure (file closure, trial, conviction/acquittal, sentencing) we first examine a general model for the entire sample. Then we examine the effect of the independent variables within several major crime categories (e.g., offenses against human life, bodily harm offenses, fraud, and economic offenses).

SAMPLE DISTRIBUTION

Ethnic and Gender Distribution

Our analysis at this stage relates to the files of the 24,984 subjects—76.62 percent Jews (N =19,932) and 23.38 percent Israeli Arabs (N =5,592) (see Table 4). Arabs constitute about 18 percent of Israel's total population. However, the average size of a household in the Arab sector is larger than in the Jewish sector due to their larger number of children per household; thus, the proportion of adult Arabs in the general population is somewhat lower (around 16%). The gender distribution in the total sample was 85.2 percent males and 14.8 percent females. Among the males, 74.35 percent were Jews and 25.65 percent were Arabs. Among the females, 88.3 percent were Jews and 11.7 percent were Arabs. Among the Jews in the sample, 16.8 percent were females and among the Arabs, 7.7 percent were females.

Of the total 60,018 files opened against Jews and Israeli Arabs in our sample, 21.57 percent were against Arabs and 78.43 percent against Jews. Breakdown by gender and nationality reveals a similar pattern. Of all male files, 24.6 percent were against Arabs and 75.4 percent against Jews. Of the female files, 8.2 percent were against Arabs and 91.8 percent against Jews.

Age Distribution and Marital Status

The sample population was divided into five age categories: *(1)* under twenty-one (5.3%); *(2)* twenty-one to thirty (33.7%); *(3)* thirty-one to forty (30%); *(4)* forty-one to fifty (16.9%); and *(5)* fifty-one and over (14.1%).

The average age of the Jewish subjects was 26.26 and of the Arabs, 22.55. The average age of the males was 25.47 among the Jews and 22.13 among the Arabs. Of the females, the average age was 29.67 among the Jews and almost the same (29.04) among Arabs. The majority of the subjects (62.3%) were married and the remainder (37.7%) either single or widowed.

Distribution of Files

Table 3 shows the distribution of files by offense category and nationality (Jews and Israeli Arabs). As already stated, the research population consisted of subjects apprehended for a first offense between 1980 and 1990. This gave us a total of 60,018 files. Because our data is cumulative, all subsequent files opened against these same subjects up to the year 1992 were recorded. Thus, those subjects who entered the criminal justice system in 1980 had more time to accumulate files than those premiering in the latter part of the study period.

The number of files per subject does not coincide with number of convictions per subject—many files were closed before reaching the judicial stage. However, they do represent contacts with the police and law enforcement agencies. Of the total number of files, 84 percent pertained to males, 78 percent to Jews and 22 percent to Arabs.

Distribution of Offenses

The proportion of Arabs in our sample is higher than in the general population and, therefore, it would seem that Arabs have a higher probability of generating criminal files than Jews. Let us examine the distribution of offenses in our population sample and thereby ascertain, among other things, whether this overrepresentation of Arabs might not be due to higher participation in specific offense categories.

Security Offenses

This category includes offenses such as: treason and espionage, rebellion and plotting against the state, violation of emergency rules (carried over from the time of the British mandate), infiltration across the border to commit sabotage, and violation of the Official Secrets Act. Jews, who constitute about 77 percent of the research sample, account for 43 percent of the security offenses and Arabs, about 56 percent (more than twice their rate in the sample). However, security offenses account for only 1.28 percent of all offenses in our sample and have been committed during the period covered by the study (see table 3). This low rate is mainly due to the exclusion of all files handled by the military courts. For Jews, this category includes elimination of only 5 percent of all security offenses, but for Arabs, 95 percent of the files opened against them for security offenses were excluded. Most of the offenses in this category are grouped together and listed as "other offenses against the security of the state" without specifying further details. Of the 770 files related to security matters, 54 percent pertained to this category—Jews 60 percent, and Arabs 40 percent. This category accounts for 0.71 percent of the offenses among the Jews and 3.9 among the Arabs.

Table 3
Distribution of Files by Nationality (for Jews and Arabs)

Type of Offense	Jews	Arabs	Total
Security	**335** 43.51[1] *0.71*[2]	**435** 56.49 *3.90*	**770** 1.28
Public Order	**10,560** 77.22 *22.43*	**3,116** 22.78 *24.07*	**13,676** 22.79
Against Person	**115** 35.28 *0.24*	**211** 64.72 *1.60*	**326** 0.54
Against Body	**6,545** 76.24 *13.90*	**2,040** 23.76 *15.76*	**8,585** 14.30
Sex Offenses	**655** 81.57 *1.39*	**148** 18.43 *1.14*	**803** 1.34
Vice Offenses	**3,918** 84.44 *8.32*	**722** 15.56 *5.58*	**4,640** 7.73
Property Offenses	**18,617** 77.75 *39.55*	**5,328** 22.25 *41.15*	**23,945** 39.90
Fraud Offenses	**4,914** 87.44 *10.44*	**706** 12.56 *5.45*	**5,620** 9.36
Economic Offenses	**700** 87.90 *1.49*	**96** 12.10 *0.74*	**796** 1.32
Administrative Offenses	**45** 46.39 *0.09*	**52** 53.61 *0.4*	**97** 0.16
Licensing Offenses	**343** 87.94 *0.72*	**47** 12.05 *0.36*	**390** 0.64
Other	**324** 85.56 *0.78*	**46** 12.43 *0.35*	**370** 0.61
Total	**47,071** 78.43	**12,947** 21.57	**60,018** 100

1. Row percentage
2. Percent from total number of records

Public Order Offenses

Public order offenses account for 23 percent of all offenses in our sample. This offense category includes causing a disturbance in public, rioting, assaulting a police officer, failure to cooperate with a police officer on duty, causing a public nuisance, blocking the right of way, trespassing, illegal assembly or organization, causing a disturbance in a public institution, bribery, illegal games and gambling, and so on. The distribution of offenses by nationality in this category corresponds closely to the proportion of Jews and Arabs in the overall study population (see table 3). The most frequent offense (20%) is "threatening conduct" (Jews 84%, Arabs 6%), followed by, in descending order: "offenses against the judicial system" (Jews 82%, Arabs 18%), and "causing disturbance in public institution" (Jews 65%, Arabs 35%).

Offenses Against Person

This category includes crimes such as homicide, attempted homicide, manslaughter, threat of homicide, and since 1988, following the onset of the Intifada, rock-throwing for nationalistic purposes. The clear difference in the representations of Jews and Arabs in this crime category (35.28% and 64.72%, respectively) may be due to the increase in the incidence of "rock-throwing for nationalistic purposes" during the period covered by the study. It is surprising that Intifada actions hardly spilled over into the Israeli Arab population (with only six rock-throwing files in our Arab sample). However, the high proportion of Arabs in this category is mainly due to their overrepresentation in offenses related to homicide: Of the thirty-two homicide files in our sample, twenty-one (65.6%) were against Arabs (their proportion in the overall sample, 22%), compared to eleven (34.4%) against Jews. It is also interesting to note that none of the Arab women had homicide files, whereas women accounted for four out of the eleven Jewish homicide files. If nothing else, this is indicative of the difference between the two communities with regard to the status of women.

Offenses Against Body

Included in this category are offenses such as: causing bodily harm, assault, criminal negligence, kidnapping and illegal confinement, throwing an incendiary bottle (T.I.B.), tire-burning, erecting barriers, and so on. One might wonder about the logic of classifying rock-throwing in the "offenses against human life" category and T.I.B. in the less-serious category of "bodily harm offenses," assuming that the consequences of the latter are potentially more injurious than the former. However, T.I.B. and tire-burning (both offenses associated with the Intifada), occur relatively infrequently, at least within the borders of Israel and, as such, they had a very marginal effect on the total number of files in the "bodily harm" category. As expected, Arabs were represented more frequently in offenses with a nationalistic background, such as throwing incendiary bottles (thirteen cases, all Israeli Arabs), erecting barriers (91%, Israeli Arabs), and tire-burning.

Property Offenses

More than 21 percent of the property offense files are for "breaking and entering" (into private homes and businesses)—Jews about 84 percent and Arabs 16 percent. Two other frequent offenses in this category are "car theft" and "theft from a vehicle," with a total of 4,168 files in our sample (Jews 76% and Arabs, 24%).

Other Offenses

The 4640 files in the "vice" category include procurement, soliciting for the purpose of prostitution, running a brothel, and seducing or soliciting minors. Of these, 84.44 percent were against Jews and 15.56 percent against Arabs. Significant underrepresentation of Arabs (in relation to their proportion in the general population) is observed in the "fraud and economic offenses" category. Of the 5,620 files for fraud, Jews accounted for 87.44 percent and Arabs 12.56 percent. A similar picture is obtained for "economic offenses"—out of 796 files, Jews accounted for 87.9 percent and Arabs 12.1 percent. The underrepresentation of Arabs in these categories probably reflects their lower rate of participation in the business sector and white-collar occupations.

Recidivism

We define recidivism in terms of number of files accumulated by a subject over the period covered by the study rather than number of convictions. However, the subjects of the research sample entered the criminal justice system at different points in time and, therefore, the probability of being defined a recidivist in this study varies. Subjects with a first file in 1980 had a much higher probability of being defined a recidivist than those with a first file ten years later, in 1990. Thus, recidivism here reflects all recorded contacts with the criminal justice system, from apprehension by the police and investigation as a suspect, onwards. In order to prevent inflation of the recidivism rates, when there was more than one entry on the same date (assuming that more than one file on the same day relates to one and the same event), only the most serious one was counted as an event and included in the study. Recidivism was ranked as follows: *0,* no prior file; *1,* one previous file; *2,* two previous files; *3+,* three or more prior files.

The data presented in table 4 reveals that the distribution of Jews and Arabs is very similar at each level of recidivism and that the contribution of the two national groups tends to be proportional to their size in the overall sample.

Table 4
Distribution of Recidivism by Nationality

Number of Prior Criminal Files	Jews	Arabs	Total
0	**10,839**	**2,903**	**13,796**
	78.96[1]	21.04	55.22
	54.30[2]	*51.90*	
1	**3,281**	**1,027**	**4,308**
	76.16	23.84	17.24
	16.40	*18.30*	
2	**1,521**	**530**	**2,051**
	74.16	25.84	8.21
	7.60	*9.40*	
3+	**3,697**	**1,132**	**4,829**
	76.56	23.44	19.33
	18.50	*20.20*	
Total	**19,932**	**5,592**	**24,984**
	76.62	23.38	

1. Row percentage
2. Column Percentage

With regard to gender and recidivism, Jews and Arabs exhibit a similar pattern. Most subjects, and especially women, had no previous file (category *0*). The proportion of males and females in recidivism categories *1* and *2* is about the same. However, males feature more frequently among the more serious recidivists (category *3*) than females (males 20.82%, females 14.42%). In the male population, 43.36 percent had no prior file and 20.84 percent had three or more prior files. In the female population, more than 60 percent had no prior file, 16.26 percent had one prior file, 8.04 percent had two prior files, and 14.42 had three or more prior files.

Gender and Criminality

It is not often that one has the opportunity to examine patterns of offenses by gender and national or ethnic group. Let us first compare female criminality along the national dimension. The picture obtained for Jewish women best fits the established image of female criminality—25 percent of the files opened for Jewish women were for property offenses, 18 percent fraud, 28.5 percent for public order offenses, 16 percent for offenses involving violence such as causing bodily harm, and about 10 percent for crimes against morality (vice category). The picture obtained for Israeli Arab women is somewhat different: 31 percent

Table 5
Offense Files by Gender and Nationality

Offenses	Male Jews	Male Arabs	Male Total	Female Jews	Female Arabs	Female Total
Security	**347**[1]	**494**	**841**	**32**	**36**	**68**
	41[2]	59	*1.6*[3]	47	53	*.7*
Public Order	**8,161**	**2,954**	**11,115**	**2,553**	**236**	**2,789**
	73	27	*21.7*	92	8	*28.6*
Against Person	**104**	**220**	**327**	**15**	**7**	**22**
	33	67	*.6*	68	32	*.2*
Against Body	**5,227**	**1,909**	**136**	**1,435**	**183**	**1,618**
	73	27	*13.9*	89	11	*16.6*
Sex Offenses	**653**	**152**	**805**	**5**	**0**	**5**
	81	19	*1.6*	100	0	*.05*
Vice Offenses	**3,027**	**694**	**3,721**	**899**	**40**	**939**
	81	19	*7.3*	96	4	*9.6*
Property Offenses	**16,574**	**5,223**	**21,797**	**2,211**	**244**	**2,455**
	76	24	*42.5*	90	10	*25.2*
Fraud	**3,303**	**695**	**3,998**	**1,635**	**33**	**1,668**
	83	17	*7.8*	98	2	*17.1*
Economic Crimes	**638**	**109**	**747**	**67**	**12**	**79**
	85	15	*1.5*	85	15	*.8*
Administration	**44**	**53**	**97**	**2**	**2**	**4**
Offenses	45	55	*.2*	50	50	*.04*
License Offenses	**301**	**36**	**356**	**28**	**1**	**29**
	89	11	*.7*	97	3	*.3*
Other	**293**	**63**	**356**	**81**	**2**	**83**
	82	18	*18*	98	2	*.85*
Total	**38,675**	**12,602**	**51,277**	**8,963**	**796**	**9,759**
	75.4	*24.6*	*100*	*91.8*	*8.2*	*100*

1. *N*
2. Row percentage
3. Column percentage

of their files were for property offenses, none were for sex crimes, and only 5 percent were for crimes against morality. However, 23 percent of the files opened for Arab women were for violent crimes such as "causing bodily harm," as opposed to 16 percent among Jewish women. The proportion of files for public order offenses was also higher among the Arab women (30%). Files for security offenses were relatively rare among Jewish females (0.4%) and significantly higher among Arab females (4.5%).

To sum up the differences between the distribution of offense categories among Jewish and Arab women, it seems that the Arab women were proportionally less involved in criminal activity—almost 92 percent of all files opened against females pertained to Jewish women. However, only in the fraud category was their proportion much higher than their proportion in the female sample population (Jews 98%, Arabs only 2%). Arab women were overrepresented in property offenses, public order offenses, and causing bodily harm (see table 5).

As far as male criminality is concerned, the most common offense category among men, both Jews and Arabs, was the "property offense" category (42.5% of all male offenses: Jews 48.8%, Arabs 41%). This was followed by, in descending order, "public order offenses" (21.7% of all male offenses: Jews 21.1%, Arabs 23.4%); "fraud" (7.8% of all male offenses: Jews 8.5%, Arabs 5.5%); "causing bodily harm" (13.9% of all male files: Jews 13.5%, Arabs 15.1 percent).

Our next step was to perform a multivariate analysis in order to arrive at a better understanding of how the various legal and extralegal variables interact and affect the decisions at each juncture of the criminal justice system. This analysis is described in the next chapter.

NOTE

1. This would be similar to what is known in North America as "arrest records."

4

At the Mercy of the Israeli Criminal Justice System

So far, we have a fair idea as to the distribution of the criminal investigation files opened against the subjects of our sample. The opening of a file by the police is the first step into the criminal justice system. Following investigation, the police will decide whether to recommend prosecution or close the file and thereby terminate all criminal proceedings. The police recommendation is then passed on to the prosecutor who, in turn, will independently decide whether to accept or reject it.

FILE CLOSURE

On what grounds can a file be closed? Do extralegal factors come into play in arriving at a file closure decision? Do disparities exist between various sectors of the populations? If so, who is most likely to benefit from file closure? An attempt is made here to construct a statistical model which will incorporate the legal and extralegal variables that best explain file closure decisions by the police and the prosecutor.

Out of a total number of 61,711 files, 25,183 (41.95%) were closed and criminal proceedings terminated. Two major factors account for the closure of 97.25 percent of these files: the first, insufficient evidence (48.40%), and the second, lack of public interest (48.85%). All other grounds for file closure account for less than 1 percent each, and together add up to a mere 2.75 percent of the total number of files, therefore receiving limited consideration in the analysis.

The proportion of closures out of all files closed (78.40% for Jews and 20.60% for Arabs) deviates only slightly from the representation of these two populations in the research sample (Jews 78% and Arabs 22%). Overall—over time and across offenses—Jews have a slightly better chance of having their files closed than Arabs (42% and 39%, respectively). This suggests that the probability of file closure is only marginally better for Jews than Arabs. This difference does not seem to be substantively significant. However, when file closure is examined by type of offense (see table 6), our data indicate that with the exception of one crime category (economic offenses), the proportion of files closed is higher for Jews than Arabs. This disparity is especially marked in the case of offenses against human life. In the case of property offenses, on the other hand, the proportion of file closures among Jews and Arabs is almost identical.

Table 6
Distribution of File Closure by Offense Category and Nationality

File Closure Offense Category	**Jews (%)**	*N*	**Arabs (%)**	*N*
Security Offenses	46.97	379	35.28	530
Public Order	46.78	10,714	39.94	3,190
Against Human Life	47.54	122	25.11	227
Bodily Harm	49.71	6,662	47.32	2,092
Sex Offenses	48.33	658	35.53	152
Vice	32.17	3,926	29.16	734
Property Offenses	37.83	18,785	37.66	5,467
Fraud	46.96	4,938	36.13	728
Economic Offenses	17.73	705	24.79	121
Administrative	45.65	46	30.91	55
Licensing Offenses	48.02	329	29.73	37
Other	36.90	374	29.23	65
Total	**20,008** **42.00%**	**47,638**	**5,175** **39.00%**	**13,398**

The decision to close a file is dependent on a variety of factors, such as age, type of offense and prior conviction (table 6), all of which are included in the multivariate analysis described below.

MULTIVARIATE ANALYSIS: LOGISTIC REGRESSION

The effect of the various independent variables on file closure was examined using a logistic regression procedure with the parameters of the model estimated by the maximum-likelihood method. The unstandardized parameter estimates of the general model shown in table 7 indicate that "being an Arab" as opposed to "being a Jew" results in a lower likelihood of file closure, where Jews constitute the omitted category in the analysis. Table 7 also shows that "being a male" and "being older" both result in reduced likelihood of file closure. It is interesting to note that as we move along the decade covered by our study, the likelihood of file closure increases.

Applying equations (1) and (2) (presented in chapter 3) to the findings in table 7 reveals that the probability of file closure for an Arab age twenty-five with no prior criminal file is .35, and for a Jew with the same profile it is .37 (period 1). This probability increases towards the end of the decade (period 6), reaching .61 for Jews and .59 for Arabs (see table 8).

Table 7
Logistic Regression for File Closure: General Model

Variable	Parameter Estimate	Standard Error	Wald chi-square	pr > Wald χ^2
Intercept	-0.736	0.043	334.27	0.0001
Arab	-0.090	0.021	17.036	0.0001
Recidivism	-0.301	0.008	1386.45	0.0001
Age	0.016	0.0009	307.68	0.0001
Family Status	0.114	0.019	35.70	0.0001
Prior Prison Sentence	0.059	0.034	2.94	N.S.
Prior Convictions	-0.041	0.002	204.20	0.0001
Sex	-0.180	0.024	56.30	0.0001
Period 2	0.643	0.032	390.59	0.0001
Period 3	0.712	0.032	616.40	0.0001
Period 4	0.675	0.028	576.44	0.0001
Period 5	0.819	0.027	876.02	0.0001
Period 6	0.989	0.030	1083.67	0.0001

Table 8
Predicted Probability of File Closure by Nationality, Age, and Period: General Model

	Period 1				**Period 6**			
	Jews		***Arabs***		***Jews***		***Arabs***	
	Age		**Age**		**Age**		**Age**	
	25	45	25	45	25	45	25	45
Male; no prior files	0.37	0.45	0.35	0.43	0.61	0.69	0.59	0.67
Male; 3 prior files; 1 prior conviction	0.14	0.09	0.13	0.089	0.30	0.22	0.28	0.20
Male; 5 prior files; 3 prior convictions	0.008	0.01	0.007	0.01	0.02	0.03	0.02	0.02

The probability of file closure, in the general model, for males age twenty-five with three prior files including one actual conviction is virtually identical for Jews and Arabs (.14 and .13, respectively). The likelihood of file closure decreases to .008 and .007, respectively, for Jews and Arabs age twenty-five with five prior files including three convictions (see table 8).

The findings also indicate that as long as there is no prior conviction, the probability of file closure increases from age twenty-five to age forty-five both for Jews and Arabs. However, for recidivists, the likelihood of file closure decreases with age and number of prior files.

The next stage was to examine the effects of the various independent variables on the likelihood of file closure for specific crime categories. We decided to present a selected number of offense categories, representing the most frequent and serious crimes. These categories include close to 80 percent of all offenses. Security offenses were omitted from the analysis since any comparison between Jews and Arabs would serve no serious research or theoretical purpose and teach us very little about differential processing of Jews and Arabs, as the number of Jews involved in security offenses is negligible.

Regression analysis was applied to each offense category. For this analysis, the "offenses against human life" and "bodily harm" categories were collapsed to form one "violent offense" category. Table 9 presents the results for violent offenses, table 10 for property offenses, table 11 for public order offenses, and table 12 for economic offenses.

Table 9
Logistic Regression for File Closure: Violent Offenses

Variable	Parameter Estimate	Standard Error	Wald Chi-Square	pr > Wald χ^2
Intercept	-0.503	0.100	25.05	0.0001
Arab	-0.020	0.053	0.146	N.S.
Recidivism	-0.316	-0.022	202.375	0.0001
Age	0.014	0.002	42.37	0.0001
Family Status	0.193	0.047	16.55	0.0001
Prior Prison Sentence	0.277	0.112	6.13	0.01
Prior Convictions	-0.026	0.011	5.22	0.02
Sex	-0.296	0.059	24.47	0.0001
Period 2	0.462	0.082	31.26	0.0001
Period 3	0.816	0.072	126.54	0.0001
Period 4	0.680	0.071	90.66	0.0001
Period 5	0.758	0.069	119.76	0.0001
Period 6	0.808	0.075	113.72	0.0001

Concordant = 66.4%

As can be seen from tables 9–12, the nationality variable does not have a significant effect on the likelihood of file closure. Recidivism (measured by number of files per person) was found to be the main factor in reducing the likelihood of file closure in all offense categories. In addition, file closure is more likely in the case of subjects who are older or married, and its probability increases across the ten-year period covered by the study.

Table 13 presents the results obtained after application of equations (1) and (2) to the data and calculation of the file closure probabilities for subjects with different profiles.

Table 14 shows that across all offense categories, nationality is not a significant variable in file closure—the likelihood of file closure is lower for recidivists with prior files (with or without convictions), higher among older and married subjects, and increases through the decade covered by the study (1980–1992).

Table 10
Logistic Regression for File Closure: Property Offenses

Variable	Parameter Estimate	Standard Error	Wald Chi-Square	pr > Wald χ^2
Intercept	-0.922	0.072	160.067	0.0001
Arab	-0.026	0.034	0.60	N.S.
Recidivism	-0.345	0.012	735.141	0.0001
Age	0.023	0.001	123.45	0.0001
Family Status	0.187	0.031	34.76	0.04
Prior Prison Sentence	0.146	0.052	7.93	0.004
Prior Convictions	-0.041	0.004	100.52	0.0001
Sex	-0.033	0.047	0.485	N.S.
Period 2	0.459	0.050	82.574	0.0001
Period 3	0.543	0.045	141.98	0.0001
Period 4	0.548	0.045	145.88	0.0001
Period 5	0.724	0.045	254.56	0.0001
Period 6	0.808	0.075	113.72	0.0001

Concordant = 69.2%

Table 11
Logistic Regression for File Closure: Public Order Offenses

Variable	Parameter Estimate	Standard Error	Wald Chi-Square	pr > Wald χ^2
Intercept	-0.909	0.080	128.52	0.0001
Arab	-0.245	0.045	29.65	N.S.
Recidivism	-0.198	0.017	136.436	0.0001
Age	0.017	0.001	87.06	0.0001
Family Status	0.078	0.039	4.030	0.04
Prior Prison Sentence	0.026	0.083	6.100	N.S.
Prior Convictions	-0.059	0.007	60.43	0.0001
Sex	-0.096	0.045	4.43	0.03
Period 2	0.866	0.069	157.02	0.0001
Period 3	0.859	0.060	202.19	0.0001
Period 4	0.810	0.058	192.78	0.0001
Period 5	0.931	0.056	276.35	0.0001
Period 6	0.960	0.060	250.56	0.0001

Concordant = 66.9%

Table 12
Logistic Regression for File Closure: Economic Offenses

Variable	Parameter Estimate	Standard Error	Wald Chi-Square	pr > Wald χ^2
Intercept	-0.029	0.120	0.057	N.S.
Arab	-0.330	0.085	14.78	0.0001
Recidivism	-0.315	0.026	141.58	0.0001
Age	0.001	0.002	0.18	N.S.
Family Status	-0.092	0.059	2.43	N.S.
Prior Prison Sentence	0.260	0.120	4.65	0.03
Prior Convictions	-0.070	0.010	48.52	0.0001
Sex	-0.252	0.061	16.87	0.0001
Period 2	0.652	0.098	43.86	0.0001
Period 3	0.652	0.087	55.16	0.0001
Period 4	0.564	0.084	44.61	0.0001
Period 5	0.462	0.087	27.81	0.0001
Period 6	0.980	0.094	107.96	0.0001

Concordant = 69.0%

Table 13
Predicted Probabilities for File Closure

Profile	Period1	Period 6
__Violent Offenses__		
Male; age 25	0.39	0.58
Male; age 25; 3 prior files; 1 prior conviction	0.19	0.35
Male; age 45	0.46	0.65
Male; age 45; 3 prior files; 1 prior conviction	0.24	0.42
__Public Order Offenses__		
Male; age 25	0.35	0.59
Male; age 45	0.49	0.72
Male; age 25; 3 prior files; 1 prior conviction	0.31	0.43
Male, age 45; 3 prior files; 1 prior conviction	0.29	0.52
__Property Offenses__		
Age 25	0.42	0.66
Age 25; 3 prior files; 1 prior conviction	0.20	0.40
Age 45	0.53	0.76
Age 45; 3 prior files; 1 prior conviction	0.28	0.51

In summary, nationality does not account for the differential rates of file closure in the three main offense categories. We therefore excluded this variable from the profiles. Age and prior files (with or without convictions) seem to be very important in the decision to close a file. In the case of violent and public order offenses, it is clear that older males and males without prior files have a higher chance of having their files closed. This also holds true for property offenses, where gender was not found to have an effect. In all three offense categories, the chances of file closure increased in the latter years of the study period (the early 1990s, period 6) (see table 13).

CONVICTIONS

Following the closure of 25,183 files (41.95% of the sample), 35,242 were turned over for further judicial processing (trial). Out of these, 19,320 (54.82%) resulted in a conviction. Differential conviction rates for Jews and Arabs suggest that there is more discrimination at the conviction level than at the file closure level. Out of all convictions, 74.40 percent were of Jews, and 25.60 percent of Arabs (who constitute 23% of the total sample). In fact, out of all Jewish files referred to court, conviction was reached in 53 percent of the cases, whereas among Arabs the rate of conviction was 61 percent.

TYPE OF OFFENSE, NATIONALITY, AND CONVICTION RATE

Property offenses accounted for most of the convictions (38%) followed by, in descending order: public order offenses (23%), causing bodily harm (12%), fraud (10.50%), and vice offenses (9%). Together, these offense categories accounted for 92.50 percent of the total number of convictions, with none of the other offense categories exceeding 2.50 percent of all convictions.

The overrepresentation of Arabs in convictions is especially marked in low-volume offense categories. These less-frequent offenses are often more serious, as in the case of security offenses or offenses against human life, where the Arab contribution is 62 percent and 76 percent, respectively, of all convictions. Arabs are also overrepresented in the sex offense category, accounting for 30 percent of all convictions.

Arabs are only slightly overrepresented in the more common offense categories, such as public order offenses (28%), causing bodily harm (27%), and property offenses (27%), compared to their share in the number of files referred to court. In the vice, fraud, and economic offense categories, they are noticeably underrepresented (19%, 15%, and 12%, respectively) (see table 14).

Examination of the distribution of convictions by nationality (column distribution) shows the property offense category to be the modal convicted followed by, in descending order: public order offenses (Jews 22.60%, Arabs 25.30%), and causing bodily harm (Jews 11.80%, Arabs 12.90%). These three offense categories account for over 70 percent of all convictions in both national groups, their rank order and frequency are similar. It is in the low-volume but more serious offense categories that more salient differences are found—convictions in the "offenses against the human life" category make up 2.20 percent of total Arab convictions, compared to only 0.20 percent of the Jewish. Similarly, and not surprisingly, convictions for security offenses constitute 2.80 percent of all convictions among Arabs and only 0.60 percent among Jews (see column percents in table 14).

Table 14
Distribution of Convictions by Offense Category and Nationality

Offense Category	Jews *n*	Arabs *n*	Total *n* (%)
Security Offenses	**86**	**140**	**226**
	38[1]	62	(1.2)
	0.6[2]	*2.8*	
Public Order Offenses	**3,192**	**1,250**	**4,442**
	72	28	(23)
	22.6	*25.3*	
Offenses Against Human Life	**35**	**110**	**145**
	24	76	(0.8)
	0.2	*2.2*	
Bodily Harm	**1,694**	**641**	**2,335**
	73	27	(12.1)
	11.8	*12.9*	
Sex Offenses	**150**	**65**	**215**
	70	30	(1.1)
	1.0	*1.3*	
Vice	**1,396**	**336**	**1,732**
	81	19	(9)
	9.7	*6.8*	
Property Offenses	**5,379**	**1,969**	**7,348**
	73	27	(38)
	37.4	*39.8*	
Fraud	**1,723**	**298**	**2,021**
	85	15	(10.5)
	12.0	*6.0*	
Economic Offenses	**425**	**57**	**482**
	88	12	(2.5)
	3.0	*1.1*	
Administrative Offenses	**16**	**31**	**47**
	34	66	(0.2)
	0.1	*0.6*	
Licensing Offenses	**137**	**19**	**156**
	88	12	(0.8)
	0.9	*0.3*	
Other	**137**	**34**	**171**
	80	20	(0.9)
	0.9	*0.7*	
Total	**14,370**	**4,950**	**19,320**
	74.4	25.6	(100)

1. Row percentage
2. Column percentage

GENDER, NATIONALITY, AND CONVICTION

Male Convictions

Males account for 84 percent of all files and this proportion remains almost the same (84.80%) at the conviction level. However, following trial, the proportion of Arab males convicted increases from 23 percent of all files to 28.60 percent of all convictions. Arab overrepresentation is most marked in convictions for security offenses, public order offenses, crimes against human life, causing bodily harm, sex offenses, and property offenses. They are underrepresented in the vice, fraud, and economic offense categories.

The marked overrepresentation in the conviction rates of Arab males might lead to claims of differential treatment by nationality. Examination of male conviction rates by offense and nationality shows that the most frequently convicted offenses are property offenses (40% of all convicted offenses among Jews and Arabs), followed by, in descending order: public order offenses (Jews 20.60%, Arabs 25.10%), and causing bodily harm (Jews 11.30%, Arabs 12.70%) (see table 15).

Female Convictions

Females account for 16 percent of all files in the sample and 15.20 percent of all convictions. Arab women contributed 9.20 percent (N = 272) to the total female conviction rate, which constitutes a mere 1.40 percent of the total number of convictions (male and female).

Examination of the female conviction rates by offense category and nationality (excluding low-volume categories) reveals that Arab females are overrepresented in crimes against human life and property offenses, and underrepresented in vice, fraud, and economic offenses. The results also show that Jewish females are convicted mainly for public order offenses (29%), followed by, in descending order: property offenses (25%), and fraud (20.90%). Arab females tend to be convicted mainly for property offenses (37.90%), followed by, in descending order: public order offenses (30.10%), and causing bodily harm (18%) (see table 15).

A logistic regression analysis was performed to identify the variables that affect conviction, and offender profiles were examined for their contribution to the conviction outcome.

MULTIVARIATE ANALYSIS: LOGISTIC REGRESSION

The multivariate logistic regression analysis included all of the legal variables (e.g., prior police file, prior conviction, and prior prison sentence) as well as the extralegal variables (e.g., nationality, gender, age, and the period of the

Table 15
Distribution of Convictions by Offense Category, Gender, and Nationality

	Males			Females		
Offense Category	**Jews**	**Arabs**	**Total**	**Jews**	**Arabs**	**Total**
	n	***n***	***n***	***n***	***n***	***n***
Security Offenses	**82**	**136**	**218**	**4**	**4**	**8**
	38[1]	62	1.3	50	50	1.3
	0.7[2]	*2.9*		*0.1*	*1.5*	
Public Order	**2,417**	**1,168**	**3,585**	**775**	**82**	**857**
	67	33	21.9	90	10	29.1
	20.6	*25.1*		*29.0*	*30.1*	
Against Human Life	**32**	**109**	**141**	**3**	**1**	**4**
	23	77	0.9	75	25	0.1
	0.2	*2.3*		*0.1*	*0.4*	
Bodily Harm	**1,324**	**592**	**1,916**	**370**	**49**	**419**
	69	31	1.2	88	12	14.2
	11.3	*12.7*		*13.8*	*18.0*	
Sex Offenses	**150**	**65**	**215**	**0**	**0**	**0**
	70	30	1.3			
	1.3	*1.4*				
Vice	**1,168**	**317**	**1,485**	**228**	**19**	**247**
	79	21	9.1	92	8	8.4
	10.0	*6.8*		*8.5*	*7.0*	
Property Offenses	**4,711**	**1,866**	**6,577**	**668**	**103**	**771**
	72	28	40.2	87	13	26.2
	40.3	*40.1*		*25.0*	*37.9*	
Fraud	**1,165**	**288**	**1,453**	**558**	**10**	**5,688**
	80	20	8.9	98	2	19.3
	9.9	*6.2*		*20.9*	*3.7*	
Economic Offenses	**401**	**55**	**456**	**24**	**2**	**26**
	88	12	2.8	92	8	0.9
	3.4	*1.2*		*0.9*	*0.7*	
Administrative	**15**	**30**	**45**	**1**	**1**	**2**
	33	67	0.3	50	50	0.07
	0.1	*0.6*		*0.03*	*0.4*	
Licensing Offenses	**123**	**19**	**142**	**14**	**0**	**14**
	87	13	0.9	100		0.5
	1.0	*0.4*		*0.5*		
Other	**107**	**33**	**140**	**30**	**1**	**31**
	76	24	0.8	97	3	1.1
	0.9	*0.7*		*1.1*	*0.4*	
Total	**11,695**	**4,678**	**16,373**	**2,675**	**272**	**2,947**
	100.0	100.0	100.0	100.0	100.0	100.0

1. Row percentage
2. Column percentage

conviction) of the study. Here, too, the two offense categories, "offenses against human life" and "bodily harm," were collapsed to give one "violent offense" category.

General Model

The first run was conducted on the overall convicted population without controlling for type of offense in order to investigate the effect of the extralegal variables (nationality, age, and period) and the legal variables (number of files and prior convictions). In order to limit the vast number of profiles that would otherwise be generated, it was assumed for the purpose of the analysis, that all subjects are male and unmarried, with no prior prison record.

From the profiles obtained (table 16), it becomes quite clear that the likelihood of Arabs being convicted is higher than that of Jews. In general, the disparity, which fluctuates between .6 and .15, depending on conviction period and specific profile, is significant not only statistically, but also substantively (the results for the regression analysis are presented in table 1 of the appendix). The results here are systematic and consistent across time periods, level of recidivism (number of prior files and convictions), and age.

Another very interesting observation is that the likelihood of a conviction increases dramatically in the early 1990s (period 6) compared to the early 1980s (period 1). Here, too, the increase is significant both statistically and substantively, with the increased likelihood of conviction sometimes reaching 400 percent or more for certain profiles. Note also that the discrepancy between conviction rate of Jews and Arabs increases across the ten-year period of the study.

The association between conviction rate and prior file (with or without conviction) is disturbing in view of the fact that, formally, the conviction profiles should not reflect the number of prior files or convictions. Neither should play a statistically significant role in the conviction stage because, according to Israeli judicial procedure, reference to prior files and convictions takes place only after the current conviction, in the sentencing stage.

Violent Offenses

In the case of violent offenses, Arabs seem to have a greater chance of being convicted than Jews. This tendency is consistent regardless of number of previous files or convictions (see regression in table 2 of the appendix). In addition, the conviction rate increases markedly in the later years of the study period; this holds true for all offenders, Jews and Arabs alike. Table 17 shows that the older the subject, the higher the likelihood of conviction. This tendency holds true also for Jews and Arabs. We also find that the age effect persists even if the number of prior files and convictions is controlled.

Table 16
Predicted Probability for Conviction by Period: General Model

Profile	Period 1	Period 6
Male; Arab; young;[1] no prior files; no prior convictions	0.20	0.81
Male; Jew; young; no prior files; no prior convictions	0.12	0.69
Male; Arab; young; 3 prior files; 1 prior conviction	0.19	0.79
Male; Jew; young; 3 prior files; 1 prior conviction	0.10	0.67
Male; Arab; young; 5 prior files; 3 prior convictions	0.19	0.80
Male; Jew; young; 5 prior files; 3 prior convictions	0.11	0.66
Male; Arab; old;[2] no prior files; no prior convictions	0.40	0.91
Male; Jew; old; no prior files; no prior convictions	0.25	0.84
Male; Arab; old; 3 prior files; 1 prior conviction	0.36	0.90
Male; Jew; old; 3 prior files; 1 prior conviction	0.22	0.82
Male; Arab; old; 5 prior files; 3 prior convictions	0.38	0.91
Male; Jew; old; 5 prior files; 3 prior convictions	0.25	0.85

1. Young refers to subjects age 25.
2. Old refers to subjects age 45.

Table 17
Predicted Probability for Conviction in Violent Offenses by Period

Profile	Period 1	Period 6
Arab; young;[1] male; no prior files; no prior convictions	0.21	0.78
Jew; young; male; no prior files; no prior convictions	0.12	0.63
Arab; young; male; 5 prior files; 3 prior convictions	0.31	0.86
Jew; young; male; 5 prior files; 3 prior convictions	0.18	0.75
Arab; old;[2] male; no prior files; no prior convictions	0.37	0.90
Jew; old; male; no prior files; no prior convictions	0.22	0.80
Arab; old; male; 5 prior files; 3 prior convictions	0.50	0.93
Jew; old; male; 5 prior files; 3 prior convictions	0.33	0.87

1. Young refers to subjects age 25.
2. Old refers to subjects age 45.

Public Order Offenses

The pattern obtained for public order offenses is almost identical to that of the general model and the violent offenses model. Again, Arabs have a higher probability to be convicted. This result is consistent across all profiles tested (see table 18), and this tendency is also much higher in the 1990s (period 6) than at the beginning of the research period. Again, the conviction rate increases with the age of the subject (for findings of the regression analysis, see table 3 of the appendix).

Property Offenses

The conviction rate for property offenses varies by nationality, age, and period (see regression in table 4 of the appendix). Arabs have a higher chance of being convicted in each profile presented and in each of the time periods. We also see (table 19) that the likelihood of conviction increases with recidivism (although this ought not to be a factor in the presentencing stage), and age. The increase in the tendency to convict in the latter period is very dramatic. However, although convictions (both Jews and Arabs) increase from period 1 to period 6, the discrepancy between the two national groups decreases.

Table 18
Predicted Probability for Conviction in Public Order Offenses by Period

Profile	Period 1	Period 6
Arab; young;[1] male; no prior files; no prior convictions	0.42	0.89
Jew; young; male; no prior files; no prior convictions	0.28	0.81
Arab; young; male; 5 prior files; 3 prior convictions	0.35	0.77
Jew; young; male; 5 prior files; 3 prior convictions	0.22	0.64
Arab; old;[2] male; no prior files; no prior convictions	0.57	0.94
Jew; old; male; no prior files; no prior convictions	0.42	0.86
Arab; old; male; 5 prior files; 3 prior convictions	0.50	0.86
Jew; old; male; 5 prior files; 3 prior convictions	0.34	0.76

1. Young refers to subjects age 25.
2. Old refers to subjects age 45.

Table 19
Predicted Probability for Conviction in Property Offenses by Period

Profile	Period 1	Period 6
Arab; young;[1] no prior convictions	0.26	0.85
Jew; young; no prior convictions	0.15	0.75
Arab; young; 3 prior convictions	0.32	0.90
Jew; young; 3 prior convictions	0.20	0.81
Arab; old;[2] no prior convictions	0.60	0.96
Jew; old; no prior convictions	0.46	0.93
Arab; old; 3 prior convictions	0.70	0.98
Jew; old; 3 prior convictions	0.54	0.95

1. Young refers to subjects age 25.
2. Old refers to subjects age 45.

DISCUSSION

A number of general conclusions can be drawn from our findings so far. First, Arabs clearly have a greater chance of becoming the "clients" of the criminal justice system. Israeli Arabs, who constitute about 18 percent of the total Israeli population, are overrepresented (22%) in the study sample. Assuming that our sample is random (and we have every reason to believe this to be the case), it seems that disparity exists between Arabs and Jews.

With regard to gender, Arab women are underrepresented in the total research sample as well as in the total number of female files (8.20%), whereas Arab males are overrepresented in the total number of male files (22%). This representation bias can be attributed either to discriminatory practices by the criminal justice system, or to the possibility that Arab males do commit proportionately more crimes than their Jewish counterparts.

Note, however, that the size of the disparity between Jews and Arabs in Israel is quite small in comparison to the disparity that exists in the United States between whites and African Americans (1:4 at intake, and as high as 1:9 at imprisonment).

The overrepresentation of Arabs on one hand (and we shall look mainly at the male population because they account for the overwhelming majority of the Arab files) varies across different offenses—Arabs seem to be highly overrepresented in security offenses and in offenses against human life (59% and 67%, respectively, of all files in these categories). On the other hand, they are underrepresented in sex offenses, vice, fraud, and economic offenses. This, at least in part, lends some credibility to the second possibility; namely, that Arab overrepresentation is a result of higher involvement in criminal behavior and not a consequence of discrimination. Hence our study deals with the micro level data which relates to decisions that are made with regard specific files, and the effect that nationality as well as other legal and extralegal variables have on them. These decisions should not be affected by the level of representation of either Jews or Arabs in the crime phenomenon.

File Closure

Several issues arise in analyzing the data relevant to the decision of whether to close a file or recommend prosecution. In general, a high proportion of files were closed in our sample; however, this may be misleading because this high closure rate may not reflect the actual closure rate in the general population of suspects. Recall that our sampling method introduced an equal number of first-time suspects in each year of sampling, thereby increasing their share in the population disproportionately to their actual size in the general suspect population. This point is important, because when we examine the overall file closure probability for different profiles, we find that it is more strongly affected by recidivism than nationality. The difference in the file closure probabilities of Jews and Arabs fluctuates across offenses. Nationality does not seem to be a statistically relevant variable in the three main offense categories (violent, public order, and property). The findings also show that the greater the number of prior files, the smaller the chance of file closure, and the older the suspect, the better his/her chances of file closure.

Also very striking is the consistently higher file closure rate in the early 1990s as compared to the 1980s. This increasing trend is evident in all offense categories and holds true across all profiles. This tendency could be due to more caution on the part of the police in apprehending suspects and opening files against them, and/or less rigorous legal screening of the files by the prosecution in the earlier period. Conversely, the increase in the number of file closures might be an indication of proactive enforcement on the part of the police, thereby generating an excess of "false positives" (i.e., inadequately based files with a low likelihood of obtaining a conviction), and/or increased professionalism (more rigorous screening of the files) on the part of the prosecution.

Convictions

Let us now move to the conviction phase. First, we see that the proportion of Arabs convicted increases to 25.60 percent. Recall that their share in the total study sample is 22 percent, and only 18 percent in the general population. In addition, male convictions, 29 percent of which are Arab, comprise 85 percent of all convictions. Again, it is possible that this is a reflection of discriminatory practices. However, it is equally possible that the nature of offenses committed by Arabs (and Arab males, in particular) is more serious and, therefore, more likely to result in a conviction. The overrepresentation of Arabs in convictions is not across the board. In some offense categories, Arab overrepresentation is very marked; namely, security offenses, offenses against human life, and sex offenses. On the other hand, Arabs are clearly underrepresented in convictions for vice, fraud, and economic offenses.

In all profiles examined (tables 17, 18, and 19), Arabs have a higher probability than Jews of being convicted in the more serious and frequent offenses (i.e., property offenses, offenses against public order, and crimes of violence). In addition, conviction rates are higher in the 1990s than in the 1980s. Finally, the probability of being convicted is affected by number of prior files and convictions. The finding that the higher conviction probability among recidivists is not related to nationality suggests that recidivism has a direct and independent effect, and that it does not necessarily interact with nationality. The relationship between conviction and prior files or convictions raises an important question. As noted earlier, the prior files and convictions of a defendant are made available to the judge in the sentencing stage, and not before. Therefore, prior record and conviction variables ought not to have been found significant in the regression analyses. By way of explanation, we can only suggest that, because convictions are often reached through plea bargaining, if the defendant is a recidivist and brought to trial, he/she will more readily admit to commission of the offense and, hence, be convicted. First-time defendants will be more likely to refrain from plea bargaining in the hope of being acquitted.

We have also shown that the age variable affects file closure and conviction differently. Contrary to its effect on file closure, in the conviction stage, all other factors being equal, the older the defendant, the higher the probability of a conviction.

What do our findings on file closure and conviction tell us? We have chosen to illustrate the differences in the involvement of Jews and Arabs in the two stages of file closure and conviction by using the following two figures. Figure 5 shows the differences between Jews and Arabs in the estimated probability to close a police file. The discrepancies between Jews and Arabs are quite small, and remain so for the three categories of criminal history. What is changing, though, both for Jews and Arabs, is the probability to close a police file, which declines as the number of prior records increases.

Figure 5
Estimated Probability for Closing Files Among Jews and Arabs

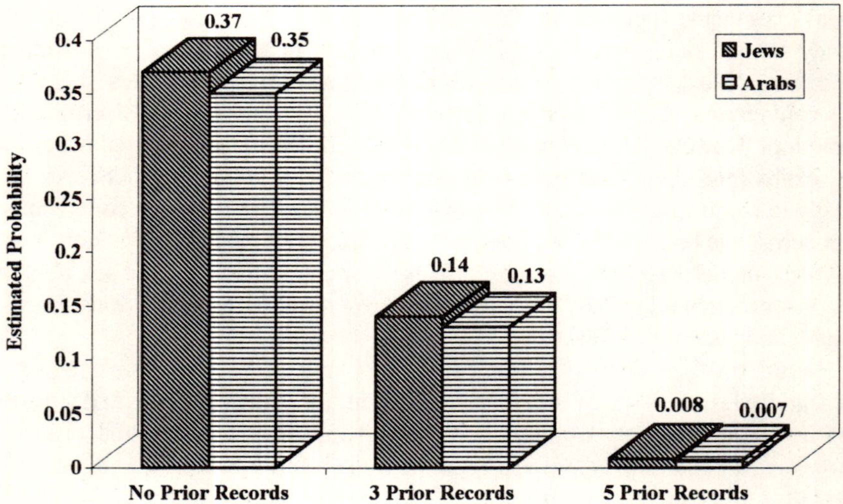

Note: Figures 5 and 6 are based on the general model in the regression analysis for period 1 and age 25.

Figure 6 illustrates the trend that takes place when decisions regarding convictions are concerned. We can clearly see that the gaps between the estimated probability of Jews and Arabs to be convicted are almost identical for the various categories of criminal history, but on the other hand, are much bigger than in the prior stage of closing files. These two figures exhibit how processing Jews and Arabs in the criminal justice system becomes more differential as suspects (or defendants) move along the process.

The seemingly opposite trends of increased file closure, together with increased likelihood of conviction in the latter period, may not be as contradictory as might appear at first glance. Proactive measures adopted by the police and increased professionalism on the part of the prosecution are quite likely to yield such a trend, which might also be attributable to social pressure on the law enforcement agencies to get tough with criminals, resulting in prompt arrests, the initiation of criminal procedures, and more convictions. Finally, it should be noted that the absolute number of criminal files opened did not change dramatically over the years. In 1980 the police generated 247,015 files, and 265,840 in 1992. In actual fact, this represents a reduction relative to the growth in Israel's adult population. In 1980 it was only 3,885,135, and in 1992 it was as high as 5,152,000. Thus, it is fair to conclude that the trends revealed in our analysis represent changes in policy due to heightened public awareness, media exposure, or fear, rather than a real increase in the crime rate.

Figure 6
Estimated Probability for Conviction Among Jews and Arabs

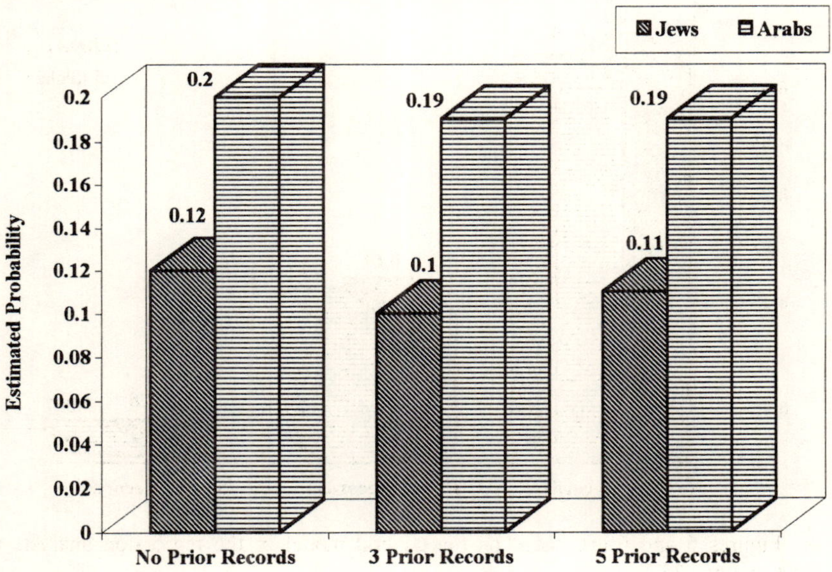

5

Doing Time

On achieving independence, not only did Israel adopt the rules of English law (Criminal Code Ordinance, 1936) as the basis for its own judicial system, it also inherited the correction facilities which became the first prisons in the state of Israel. Several changes were introduced during the early years of the state. One of these was the abolition of capital punishment for murder.[1] Today, the only crimes subject to the death penalty are "treason during wartime" and offenses under the Punishment of the Nazis and their Collaborators Law, 1950 and the Crime of Genocide Law, 1950. To date, there has been only one execution in Israel—in the case of Adolph Eichmann (the Nazi officer responsible for all transports to the death camps as part of the "Final Solution"), convicted in Israel in 1962. Thus, the prison sentence became the most severe form of punishment in the penal law, and mandatory life imprisonment replaced the death penalty in the case of a murder conviction. More recently, the Israeli legislature adopted an amendment to the penal law allowing the court discretionary power in handing down sentences of lesser severity than life imprisonment for criminal homicide.[2]

Apart from imprisonment, the main penalties imposed by courts in Israel are fines, suspended prison sentences, and probation, with the provision of imposing more than one penalty either concurrently or consecutively. For instance, a sentencing decision might include a fine and imprisonment for a determinate period, to be followed by a suspended sentence. Many criminal trials result in the imposition of a fine for offenses punishable by incarceration. Indeed, the fine is often seen as a substitute for a prison sentence. Those involved in penal policy are hardly oblivious to the clear pecuniary benefits of fining. The implementation of this penalty is relatively inexpensive and, in view of the high cost of incarceration, it represents not only a budgetary saving, but also a source of income for the state.

Fining can be perceived as indicative of liberalism in the penal policy because it seems to be negatively correlated with incarceration—quite often fluctuations in rates of imprisonment are an inverse function of parallel fluctuations in fining. Evidence from research conducted in Germany, England, and the United States has shown that, in general, incarceration rates decrease as the number of alternative penal measures increases (Bottoms 1983; Gillespie 1980). Examination of the relationship between fining and incarceration in Israel reveals that during the 1980s there was a decline in the use of fines and an increase in the rate of imprisonment.

Fining in the early 1980s, as a single penalty or in combination with other penalties, remained fairly consistent at around 67 to 68 percent. Thereafter, its relative share among all other penalties declined to 58 percent in 1988, 55 percent in 1989, and reaching as low as 49 percent in 1992 (17% as a sole penalty) (see table 20). The increasing trend of imprisonment revealed in table 20 might be an indication that Israeli society as a whole is becoming less liberal and more punitive. We also see that during the 1981-1992 period, fining (as a sole penalty or in combination with other penalties) was imposed on Arabs more often than on Jews (in 1992, 61% and 43% respectively).

Table 20
Distribution of Penalties Imposed on Convicted Offenders (1981-1992)

Penalty	1981	1985	1990	1992
Fine	67.8	67.9	49.2	29.0
Incarceration	15.7	16.2	23.4	14.0

The suspended sentence, another very common alternative to imprisonment, avoids the devastating consequences of incarceration. This is an important consideration, especially in the case of novice offenders. It is interesting to note that this penalty has been widely adopted in continental Europe, whereas in England and the United States there seems to have been more emphasis on probation. The two measures are similar in the sense that they both entail fulfillment of certain conditions. In the case of the suspended sentence, failing to fulfill these conditions (in theory) will activate the prison sentence. In Israel there seems to be a growing preference for this sentence. Suspended prison sentences, alone or combined with other penalties, comprised 47 percent of all penalties in 1981, 64 percent in 1989, and 67 percent in 1992. In 1992, suspended prison sentences were more frequent among Jews than Arabs (72% and 68%, respectively).

Probation is actually an intermediate sanction, a community alternative to imprisonment, based on the treatment model. Failure to comply with the terms of probation is an offense in itself, punishable at the discretion of the court. Probation is imposed by the courts if it is believed that community alternatives are more effective for the rehabilitation of the offender. However, more often than not, the opportunities available to the probationer in the community are totally inadequate. On the other hand, one cannot overlook the fact that probation is a more economical way of processing offenders and it avoids the negative effects of imprisonment.

Probation was implemented in Palestine by the British mandate to deal with young offenders (age nine to twenty) as part of a liberal move in 1922. It was extended to adult offenders only in 1928. As in Britain, the ordinance allowed for the imposition of probation on adult offenders for all offenses punishable by incarceration. At a later stage of the British Mandate (1937), probation was again limited, this time to males up to the age of sixteen and females up to the age of eighteen. A revision in the ordinance (1944) made adults eligible for probation. In 1964, sixteen years after the establishment of Israel, a separate adult probation service was set up. The Israeli law stipulates that the probation option must be considered in all cases involving juveniles or young adults (i.e., all convicted offenders up to the age of twenty-one). Thus, all such cases require the submission of a pre-sentencing report by the juvenile probation service.

Imprisonment for all practical purposes is the harshest of the sentences that can be imposed in Israel. The law stipulates that separate facilities be provided for males and females, pretrial detainees and convicted offenders serving prison sentences, adults and juveniles under sixteen, debtors, and first-timers. However, the facilities available allow only for partial compliance with these requirements and, in practice, separation is observed mainly between adults and juveniles, males and females, and, as far as possible, between pretrial detainees and convicted felons.

Prison sentences are prescribed and represent maximum terms which may not be exceeded. However, the courts may, at their discretion, prescribe a reduced term. Minimum sentences are restricted to a few special offenses (e.g., assaulting a police officer). If a defendant is tried for more than one charge simultaneously, separate penalties have to be pronounced for each, and the longest prison sentence will include the shorter one(s) (concurrent terms) unless the court specifies cumulative (consecutive) terms.

Our data for 1992 reveals that prison sentences were imposed most frequently for offenses against human life (62.3%) followed by security offenses (32.5%), sex offenses (31.2%), property offenses (21.7%), and assault (8.9% percent). In 1992 prison terms were imposed on about 26 percent of all adult Jewish offenders and 20 percent of all adult Arab offenders. However, only 3 percent of all prison sentences were not enjoined to other additional penalties. A differential trend is also observed when length of imprisonment is examined—Arabs tend to receive longer prison sentences (Central Bureau of Statistics, 1995). Suspended prison terms are usually imposed on top of regular prison terms, especially in bodily harm cases (58%) and cases of assault (78%).

In Israel, after serving two-thirds of a prison sentence, inmates become eligible for early release. This is usually granted as a matter of course. According to Bin-Nun, "Most offenses punishable by imprisonment are eventually requited by the payment of fines" (1992, 118).

Analysis of the distribution of the penal measures served on convicted offenders reveals a number of disparities between Jews and Arabs. Arabs constitute 25.6 percent of the convicted population of our sample. Clearly, this proportion is larger than the Arab share in the general population (18%) as well as in the overall study population (22%). Hence, if type of punishment is not affected by the nationality variable, or if the distribution of offenses is random, the proportion of Arabs within each punishment modality should be 25.6 percent, as is their share in the convicted population of our study sample. Put differently, if the distribution of the punishments deviates from 25.6 percent, one would suspect either that Arabs and Jews commit different crimes or, if the offenses are randomly distributed, that the differential distribution of penalties is attributable to differential treatment by nationality.

Table 21 reveals that three types of penalty—fine, imprisonment, and suspended sentence—account for over 97 percent of all punishments. The category "Other," which accounts for only 2.65 percent of all punishments, consists of twelve other penal measures, most of which are administrative or represent relatively light sentences, such as license revocation. Fines are imposed more frequently on Arabs than on Jews, and Arab offenders seem to receive the more "desirable" sentences—suspended prison sentence and probation—less frequently than Jews. Imprisonment seems to be shared fairly among Jews and Arabs.

Table 21
Distribution of Penalties by Nationality

Punishment	Jews	Arabs	Total
Fine	8,261	3,225	11,486
	57.65[1]	65.2	59.59
Imprisonment	3,094	1,090	4,184
	21.6	22.0	21.70
Suspended Sentence	2,444	565	3,009
	17.06	11.42	15.61
Probation	168	21	189
	1.17	0.42	0.98
All Other	363	45	404
	2.5	0.09	2.63
Total	14,330	4,946	19,276
	100	100	100

1. Column percent

Criminologists, as well as laypersons, tend to associate prior prison record with recidivism and to consider both as crucial legal factors that predict the likelihood of a prison sentence. The main focus of this chapter is the effect of prior prison record and nationality on the likelihood of receiving a prison sentence. Our analysis will attempt to ascertain whether the extralegal variable of nationality is a determinant in sentencing decisions, especially in the case of prison sentences.

Who is most likely to be sentenced to imprisonment? In this section we examine the likelihood of receiving a prison sentence for crimes of violence (the most serious offense category) and for property offenses (the most prevalent offense category). Due to their small number, and to allow for proper statistical analysis, offenses against human life were combined with bodily harm offenses to form the "violent offenses" category. A logistic regression analysis was then applied to determine which variables increase/decrease the probability of receiving a prison sentence.

GENERAL MODEL

Examination of a general model without differentiating between the various offense categories revealed that the significant variables affecting the likelihood of receiving a prison sentence are: nationality, age, marital status, gender, prior prison record, and prior convictions. The period in which the prison term was imposed follows an inconclusive pattern—some periods had a significant effect and some did not (compared to the omitted category—1980–1981) (see table 22).

Table 22
Logistic Regression for Prison Sentences: General Model, Violent Offenses, Property Offenses

Variable	General Model Parameter Estimate	Violent Offenses Parameter Estimate	Property Offenses Parameter Estimate
Arab	0.5646*	0.9239*	0.3055*
Recidivist	0.0142	0.0121	0.1759*
Age	-0.0156*	-0.9577*	-0.0060
Marital Status	-0.6635*	-0.9868*	-0.6156*
Prior Prison	3.3542*	2.8455*	3.7990*
Prior Conviction	0.0273*	0.0212	0.0237*
Gender	0.5865*	0.5348	0.6091*
Period 2	-0.4502*	-0.5164	-0.3550**
Period 3	-0.2176*	-0.9581*	-0.1980
Period 4	-0.2861*	-0.7954*	-0.1698
Period 5	-0.0961	-0.3708	-0.1493
Period 6	-0.1447	-0.7730*	-0.0263
Intercept	-2.2794	-0.9511	-2.9289
-2 Log L	12389.62	1292.42	4408.61
χ^2	9840.37	9840.37	9840.37
df.	12	12	12
p	0.001	0.001	0.001

* $p < .01$; ** $p < .05$

Table 22 presents the respective columns with the parameter estimates showing the variables that were significant in each logistic regression. Examination of the parameter estimates of the regressions clearly shows that prior prison record has the greatest effect on the probability of being sentenced to prison. In the case of receiving a prison sentence, the probability was calculated first by generating an average case profile and then determining the additional impact of prior prison record or nationality. This procedure involved setting all independent variables in the logistic regression equation to their sample means except for the independent variable under investigation. The unique contribution of a variable is revealed by its net effect.

It was found that a prior prison record increases the estimated probability of receiving a prison sentence to .76, and absence of a prior prison record reduces the probability of imprisonment to .09. We then applied the same procedure to the extralegal variables. It was found that when all other variables are set at their mean value, the estimated probability of Arabs receiving a prison sentence is .27 and that of Jews only .17. Calculating the probabilities on the basis of the mean values reflects the chances of the average person, Jew or Arab, i.e., mean age, mean number of prior records, to receive a prison sentence.

After examining for the effect of single variables, we attempted to create profiles representing high and low probability of receiving a prison sentence (see table 23). The profiles obtained reveal that young, unmarried, male offenders with three prior convictions and a prior prison record have the highest probability of receiving a prison sentence, and that this probability is slightly higher for Arabs than Jews (.88 and .80, respectively). The lowest probability of receiving a prison sentence is found for older, married, Jewish offenders with no prior convictions or prison record (for females, .01 and for males, .04).

Table 23
Selected Profiles of Predicted Probability of Receiving a Prison Sentence: General Model

Profile	Jews	Arabs
Young;[1] male; unmarried; prior prison; 3 prior convictions	0.80	0.88
Young; female; unmarried; prior prison; 3 prior convictions	0.69	0.80
Old;[2] male; unmarried; prior prison; 3 prior convictions	0.74	0.83
Old; female; unmarried; prior prison; 3 prior convictions	0.62	0.74
Old; male; married; no prior prison; no prior convictions	0.04	0.08
Old; female; married; no prior prison; no prior convictions	0.01	0.04

1 Young refers to age 25.
2. Old refers to age 45.

Let us now apply the model with differentiation by offense category. Again, to maintain a large enough number of subjects for the analysis, all offenses against human life and bodily harm offenses were collapsed to form one category of violent offenses. In the case of violent offenses, the parameter estimates show that prior prison record has the highest impact on the sentencing decision. Following calculation of the average case profile, the net effect of this variable was found to be .53, which means that the average offender convicted for a violent crime with a prior prison record has a 53 percent chance of receiving a prison sentence; without a prior prison record, the chance is only 5 percent. When all the other variables are set at their mean, the effect of "being an Arab" produces a probability of 13 percent, and of "being a Jew," only 5 percent.

Although, as indicated in the regression, prior prison record is the best predictor (see table 22), nationality, age, and marital status also have a significant impact on the sentencing decision in the case of violent offenders. The profiles enumerated in table 24 include those most likely, and those least likely, to lead to a term in prison.

Table 24 indicates that regardless of gender (which was not found to be significant in the regression), the likelihood of a young (twenty-five year-old) unmarried Arab with a previous prison record receiving a prison sentence is very high (.80). Another indication of the impact of prior prison record is given by the finding that the probability of receiving a prison sentence declines dramatically for Jews as well as for Arabs (.08 and .19, respectively) when there is no prior prison record. However, the difference between Jews and Arabs regarding the probability of a prison sentence remains consistent.

Table 24
Selected Profiles of Predicted Probability of Receiving a Prison Sentence: Violent Offenses

Profile	Jews	Arabs
Young;[1] unmarried; 1 prior file; 1 prior prison	0.61	0.80
Old;[2] unmarried; 1 prior file; 1 prior prison	0.33	0.55
Young; married; 1 prior file; 1 prior prison	0.37	0.60
Old; married; 1 prior file; 1 prior prison	0.16	0.31
Young; unmarried; no prior file; no prior prison	0.08	0.19
Old; unmarried; no prior file; no prior prison	0.02	0.07
Young; married; no prior file; no prior prison	0.03	0.08
Old; married; no prior file; no prior prison	0.01	0.03

1. Young refers to age 25.
2. Old refers to age 45.

Let us now apply the analysis to property offenses to see if a similar pattern is established obtains (see table 25). The parameter estimates of the regression show that in the case of property offenses, prior prison record has the greatest impact on the chances of receiving a prison sentence. Employing the average profile procedure to determine the residual impact of prior prison record on receiving a prison sentence proves it to be very high (.81) compared to that obtained without a prior prison record (.09). Examination of the nationality variable using a similar procedure reveals that the residual effect of "being a Jew" (.24) is somewhat lower than that of "being an Arab" (.30). The logistic regression shows almost no effect for the period of sentencing, nor does the age of the offender have an impact. The rest of the variables are found to be statistically significant (see table 25). Accordingly, unmarried, Arab males with prior convictions and a previous prison record have a higher chance of receiving a prison sentence than their Jewish counterparts.

Table 25 gives the profiles with the highest and lowest probability estimates of receiving a prison sentence. It corroborates the finding that prior prison record is the most dominant variable in determining whether an offender will receive a prison sentence. Convicted offenders with the highest chance of receiving a prison sentence are unmarried males with prior police files, prior convictions, and a prior prison record (.86 for Jews, and .89 for Arabs). The probability decreases for both Jews and Arabs if the offender is married (.76 and .81, respectively) and, needless to say, decreases even further if the convicted person has no prior prison record (.07 for Jews, and .09 for Arabs).

Table 25
Predicted Probability of Receiving a Prison Sentence: Property Offenses

Profile	Jews	Arabs
Male; unmarried; 3 prior files; 3 prior convictions; 1 prior prison	0.86	0.89
Male; married; no prior file; no prior convictions.; no prior prison	0.04	0.05
Female; married; 3 prior files; 3 prior convictions; 1 prior prison	0.64	0.71
Female; married; no prior file; no prior convictions; no prior prison	0.02	0.03
Male; married; 3 prior files; 3 prior convictions; 1 prior prison	0.76	0.81
Male; married; 3 prior files; 3 prior convictions; no prior prison	0.07	0.09
Female; married; 3 prior files; 3 prior convictions; no prior prison	0.04	0.06

To sum up our findings so far, prior prison record has the strongest impact on the likelihood of receiving a prison sentence. Being single also increases the odds of getting a prison sentence. This finding is consistent across the various offense categories. Perhaps counterintuitively, gender does not significantly affect the probability of receiving a prison sentence in the case of violent offenses. It should be stressed that although Arabs stand a greater risk of being sentenced to prison, the nationality variable has a weaker impact than the systemic variable, prior prison record. It is also important to note that the combined effect of nationality and other variables fluctuates, depending on the offense. It is greater in the case of violent offenses and much smaller in the case of property crimes.

LENGTH OF SENTENCE

Having established the profiles of offenders most likely to receive a prison sentence, our next question is whether there are disparities in the length of the sentences imposed in different population groups. Our analysis takes into account the fact that our convicted offenders differ not only on extralegal variables such as age, gender, marital status, and nationality, but also on legal variables such as offense category, number of prior criminal files and convictions, and prior prison record. We entered all these independent variables in a regression analysis, with length of prison sentence as the designated dependent variable.

The first step of the analysis was designed to determine the factors affecting length of imprisonment without controlling for type of offense (table 26). The results of the multiple regression show that: (*a*) there is no significant association between nationality and length of prison sentence when all offenses are combined in one group; (*b*) the length of the prison sentence increases with age; (*c*) males tend to receive longer prison terms than females, (*d*) married offenders receive shorter terms than those who are not married, and (*e*) at the beginning of the period covered by the study (early 1980s), prison sentences are longer than later in the periods (early 1990s). Another interesting finding is the linear relationship between the length of the prison sentence and the time lag between the opening of the police file and sentencing. Contrary to the commonly held belief that postponement of the legal process is advantageous for the defendant, it appears that the longer this time lag, the longer the prison sentence.

There is also a statistically significant relationship between the number of prior files, the number of prior prison terms, and the length of the prison sentence. Paradoxically, the greater the number of police files, the shorter the sentence. However, the greater the number of prior prison terms, the longer the prison sentence incurred on the current conviction.

Table 26
Regression Coefficients for Length of Prison Sentence: General Model, Violent Offenses, Property Offenses

Variables	a General Model Beta S.E.	b Violent Offenses Beta S.E.	c Property Offenses Beta S.E.
Nationality	n.s.	n.s.	n.s.
Recidivism	-0.026*** *69.50*	n.s.	n.s.
Prior Prison Record	0.764* *9.84*	0.564* 40.74	0.744* 14.32
Age	0.081* *9.89*	n.s.	0.150* 22.78
Gender	0.077* *263.28*	n.s.	0.067* 516.52
Marital Status	-0.041* *158.58*	n.s.	-0.53** 289.14
Year of Sentence	-0.025*** 24.50	n.s.	-0.114* 41.97
Time Elapsed	0.031** 61.18	n.s.	0.051** 121.77
Intercept	1,682.80	-4,606.28	16,247
R^2	0.58	0.32	0.59

* p < .001
** p < .01
*** p < .05

Let us now examine the impact of the various variables on the length of prison sentences imposed for violent offenses. As can be seen in table 26(b), the predictability of the model (R^2) is only .32. However, the most striking finding is that the only significant variable in the regression model is number of previous prison sentences. None of the other variables (nationality, gender, marital status, age, number of prior police files) contributes significantly to the model.

In the case of property offenses, the explained variance is quite high (R^2 =.59) and a number of variables contribute significantly to the model. In fact, the only variables in the model that are not statistically significant are nationality and number of prior criminal files. On the other hand, as shown in table 26(c), number of prior convictions incurring a prison sentence and age of the offender seem to have the greatest impact on the model. It appears that married offenders receive shorter sentences for property offenses than those who are not married, and that prison terms tend to get shorter over the years of the research period. Here, too, the more drawn-out the criminal proceedings, and the longer the time lag between the opening the criminal file and sentencing, the higher the probability of a longer prison sentence.

CONCLUSIONS

It might seem logical to assume that those variables which predict the probability of receiving a prison sentence will also be good predictors of the length of the sentence imposed. This assumption is only partially supported by our findings. Prior prison record is the most significant variable in the logistic models predicting whether a convicted offender will receive a prison sentence or not. The nationality variable is also a significant predictor in both the general model and in the specific cases of violent and property offenses. However, no significant relationship was found for length of prison sentence and nationality in the general model or in the offense-specific models. Thus, although "being an Arab" increases the chances of going to prison, it does not affect the length of the sentence term. The effect of prior record on the length of the prison term is the same for Jews and Arabs.

It is interesting to note that the length of the sentence imposed for violent offenses is affected by the number of prior prison sentences; whereas gender, age, and marital status have no impact at all. This is in contrast to the findings obtained for the probability of being served a prison sentence in the first place–age was negatively related to the probability of being given a prison sentence and the younger the violent offender, the higher the chance of receiving a prison sentence. Among violent offenders, being married seems to be a "good strategy" for escaping a prison sentence. However, once sentenced to prison for a violent offense, the length of the sentence will be influenced mainly by prior prison record rather than any of the other variables that influenced the imposition of the prison sentence in the first place.

In the case of property offenses, unmarried males have a higher likelihood of receiving a prison sentence, but the longer prison sentences were imposed on older, unmarried males with a prior prison record.

The main aim of this analysis was to investigate discriminatory practices in the Israeli criminal justice system. The finding that nationality did not affect the length of the prison sentence might be interpreted as a sign of equality in sentencing. However, caution should be exercised in arriving at such a conclusion, because if the main determinant of the sentence length is number of prior prison terms, this would imply, indirectly, that there is a potential for discrimination. We have demonstrated that Arabs are more likely to receive a prison sentence than Jews; hence, they run a higher risk of accumulating a longer prison record. This indirect inference should be interpreted in light of Israel's relatively small prison population.

NOTES

1. Penal law revision (Abolition of the Death Penalty for Murder), 1954.
2. Penal law (Amendment 37),1992, Section 22(c).

6

Palestinian Offenders and Israeli Justice

BACKGROUND: ISRAEL AND THE PALESTINIANS

In May 1948, the armies of Egypt, Jordan, Syria, Lebanon, and Iraq launched a massive attack on the newly declared state of Israel. During the course of the War of Independence, and on the advice of their leaders, many Arabs fled their homes in what was known until then as Palestine, and now had become part of the new Jewish state. No one can say precisely how many Palestinian Arabs became refugees. Estimates vary considerably, according to Arab estimates, 750,000–1,000,000; Israeli estimates, about 520,000; and British estimates, 600,000–760,000 (Kimmerling and Migdal 1993). Most of the Palestinian refugees ended up in Lebanon, Egypt, and Jordan. The two largest and most densely populated areas of Palestinians were the Gaza Strip (under Egyptian rule) and the West Bank, which belonged to the Kingdom of Jordan (see map 1). Another destination, where many still reside (albeit in much smaller numbers), is Lebanon. The wealthier and better-educated Palestinians succeeded in building new lives for themselves in the capitals of the Arab world, but the less fortunate ended up in crowded refugee camps, living in deplorable conditions.

Together, the West Bank and the Gaza Strip cover an area of approximately 5,875 square kilometers. The West Bank is flanked by the River Jordan in the East, and a chain of mountains extending from north to south (Judea and Samaria), along which are located towns such as Jenin, Nablus, Ramallah, Bethlehem, and Hebron. Most of the West Bank towns are located no more than 10 to 40 kilometers from Israel's major urban centers. In contrast, the Gaza Strip is a narrow strip of land, 45 kilometers long and 5 to 12 kilometers wide, along the Mediterranean coastline, extending southward from Israel's coastal plain. Its total area is about 300 square kilometers and its population about 800,000. The population density in the Gaza Strip is about 1,730 per square kilometer, compared to about 193 in the West Bank.

About two-thirds of Gaza's population are refugees from pre–1948 Palestine, which became part of Israel. After 1948, most of the Palestinians went to live in refugee camps maintained by UNRWA (United Nations Refugee Welfare

Association) in the cities of Gaza, Kahn-Yunis, and Rafiah. Egypt did not annex the Gaza Strip. On the contrary, it maintained a policy of almost total segregation, even restricting movement in and out of the Gaza Strip to Egypt. In contrast to their brethren in the West Bank (who were granted Jordanian citizenship), Palestinians in the Gaza were denied Egyptian citizenship, forced

Map 1
Israel and the Occupied Territories: West Bank and Gaza Strip

Source: University of Haifa, Department of Geography

to retain their refugee status, and hence denied basic rights such as political participation and the opportunity to engage in institution building for themselves. Jordan, on the other hand, formally annexed the West Bank (in 1950), offering Jordanian citizenship to the refugees.

Both the West Bank and the Gaza Strip were severely lacking in both natural resources and any form of basic infrastructure. Their main source of livelihood derived from agricultural products, but their agricultural technology was largely undeveloped. This situation improved, especially in the major urban centers, due mainly to Jordanian efforts to develop economic activity and generate modest but consistent advances in the socioeconomic situation of those living in the area. However, the East Bank received preferential treatment by the Jordanian government, leaving the West Bank with its Palestinian population suffering from the harsh consequences of their dislocation, trapped in a landlocked territory.

From 1948 on, the Gaza Strip became what was essentially one big refugee camp with little prospect for change. In the West Bank, in spite of the upheavals experienced by Jordan's Palestinians, a sense of community and a degree of normalcy was retained. From time to time, its towns and villages became vibrant political arenas, with representation in the Jordanian parliament and government. Not so in Gaza, where a society emerged which has been termed a "refugee camp society" (Kimmerling and Migdal 1993). The Gaza Strip became synonymous with poverty, social misery, and despair. For many, the only source of income was the financial aid provided by UNRWA.

The 1967 Six-Day War ended in the occupation of the Golan Heights in the north (from Syria), the West Bank in the east (from Jordan), and the Gaza Strip and Sinai Peninsula in the south (from Egypt). Although Israel made it quite clear that it had no intention of returning to its 1967 borders, it also had no intention of integrating the territories and their inhabitants into the state of Israel. With no permanent solution in sight, Israel's main objective was to maintain the occupied territories as a strategic buffer zone. In order to ensure relatively normal routine under the occupation, Israel established a civil administration which operated on the basis of existing local institutions. The main advocate of this policy was Minister of Defense, Moshe Dayan the "one-eyed-general." He was also responsible for the "open bridges" policy between the West Bank and Jordan, aimed primarily at avoiding economic stagnation and depression, and based on the belief that a thriving economy was a basic necessity for maintaining tranquillity.

However, there was a wide gap between the level of the Israeli and Palestinian economies—for instance, in 1996, the value of Israeli exports alone exceeded the combined GNP (gross national product) of the West Bank and the Gaza Strip. Israel's industrial output increased fivefold between 1950 and 1966, with an impressive annual growth rate of about 9 percent. The West Bank economy was based mainly on small-scale agricultural production, whereas Israel had a highly developed and powerful agricultural business, based on sophisticated technologies, as well as a strong textile and chemical industry. Prior to 1967, Israel had been suffering a recession, but it was only temporary—following the Six-Day War, there was a tremendous economic boost, especially in the construction sector.[1] There was to be no competition between the Israeli and Palestinian economies; all financial and commercial relationships were unidirectional and one-sided. The occupied territories became an ideal market for many of Israel's industrial products, such as food, clothing, and building and construction materials. Statistics show that during the first five years of the occupation, about 12 percent of Israel's exports ended up in the occupied territories, accounting for almost 77 percent of the total imports into the territories (Central Bureau of Statistics, 1978).

One of the few commodities that the West Bank territories had to offer was cheap labor. The economy of the occupied territories, with its approximately one million inhabitants, had been heavily dependent on ties with Jordan and Egypt. These ties were cut off as a result of the Israeli occupation. In 1968, the GNP per capita was 364 IL (Israeli Lira) in the Gaza Strip, 595 IL in the West Bank, and 4,900 IL in Israel (Central Bureau of Statistics, 1978). Compared to the weak Palestinian economy, Israel's economy had entered a period of prosperity. By 1969, the unemployment rate went down to 4.5 percent and the demand for workers, especially in building and construction, agriculture, and manufacturing, grew very rapidly. This shortage of labor in certain sectors of the Israeli labor market opened a window of opportunity for many of the unemployed Palestinians. Immediately after the 1967 war, the employment of Palestinians from the occupied territories was strictly forbidden due to security considerations. By 1969, in response to pressure from the Palestinian side, the Israeli government changed its policy. However, a quota was set on the number of Palestinian workers allowed into Israel—Israeli employers were allowed to employ only those who had applied and qualified for a work permit. Very soon, the demand for cheap labor on the Israeli side, combined with desperate need for income on the Palestinian side, led to the blatant exploitation of Palestinian workers. Following the revelation that they were being underpaid—earning even less than the minimum wage—the government introduced measures to guarantee equal wages for Israeli and Palestinian workers for comparable jobs and skills. Within a short time, however, an illegal labor market emerged, with Palestinians without permits seeking to enter Israel, and Israeli employers seeking a source of cheap labor. Palestinian workers were not allowed to stay overnight in Israel; they were required by law to commute daily from their homes in the West Bank and the Gaza Strip. This resulted in many of them staying overnight illegally. Some employers cooperated, even providing shelter for their workers, in violation of the law. Farms in rural areas and construction sites in the big urban centers turned into overnight shelters for both legal and illegal Palestinian workers. Although the Palestinians became the "hewers of wood and drawers of water," their employment in Israel provided them with the means of maintaining a minimal standard of living—to bring home an income sufficient to provide for basic necessities.

Prolonged Israeli military control over the occupied territories eventually led to civil resistance, which developed into a genuine grass roots civil uprising. Once in motion, the uprising was adopted and orchestrated by the PLO (Palestine Liberation Organization), the Islamic movements, and the Popular Front for the Liberation of Palestine. These organizations worked against Israel's military forces and its civilian population.

Figures for the first years of the occupation indicate that 90 percent of offenders in Israeli prisons (both in the occupied territories and within the borders of Israel), were convicted for security offenses, and only 10 percent for conventional criminal activity (Department of Corrections, 1970). As the involvement of Palestinians in the Israeli labor market became deeper, and commuting between the occupied territories and Israel more commonplace, Palestinian involvement in criminal activity increased. Although none of the published statistical reports offer a breakdown of the offenses committed by Palestinians within the borders of the state of Israel, a few figures were provided, per our request, by the statistics division of the Israel Police Department, enabling us to examine general trends in crimes committed by Palestinians in Israel.

Out of 2,719 Palestinian offenders sentenced to prison in 1987–1988, 26 percent had committed burglary (breaking and entering), and 10 percent had been convicted for car theft or theft from a vehicle (Department of Corrections, 1987/88). Indeed, car theft quickly developed into a thriving organized industry (involving the dismantling of stolen vehicles, forging documents, resale of parts, etc.) in both the Gaza Strip and the West Bank. The open spaces along the borders made it easy to transfer stolen vehicles to the occupied territories. Many of the stolen cars were subsequently "imported" back to the Israeli market in the form of spare parts. Anecdote has it that the officers of the newly established Palestinian Police Authority drive stolen Israeli vehicles, some stolen from Israeli police officers, fully equipped with sophisticated radio and other electronic devices. This problem has featured extensively in the media due to its epidemic proportions (see, for instance *Ha'aretz*, January 12, 1989, p. 13 for an article entitled, "The Stolen Car Industry in the Occupied Territories"). Indeed, the statistics suggest that the rate of car theft in Israel is almost as high as that of the United States, and even higher than that of many European countries (in 1988, 361 vehicles per 100,000 population were stolen in Israel, 437 in the United States, and 276 in Italy).

The official crime statistics published in Israel do not have a separate breakdown of crimes committed by Palestinian Arabs within the borders of the State of Israel. Our only source regarding the share of such crimes committed is unpublished data. The overall contribution of Palestinian Arabs to criminal activity in Israel was 6 percent in 1986. These files are not truly representative of the volume of crime committed by Palestinians, because they refer only to cases for which a suspect was apprehended. The fact that the occupied territories are hostile areas does not help the Israeli police in investigating and clearing crime and, therefore, the picture obtained in table 27 probably represents only the topmost tip of the legendary iceberg. Nevertheless, the Palestinian contribution of 16 percent for sex offenses, and more than 7 percent for property offenses in the total sample of files is hardly insignificant.

Table 27
Proportion of Palestinian Files in Total Sample of Files, 1985–1986

	Year					
		1985			1986	
Offense Category	**Sample Total**[1]	**Palestinian Total**	**%**	**Sample Total**	**Palestinian Total**	**%**
Security	1,081	119	11.0	1285	110	8.5
Public Order	13,517	392	2.9	13,309	496	3.7
Human Life	321	35	10.9	371	21	5.7
Bodily Harm	8,827	256	2.9	9,323	295	3.2
Sex	1,276	157	12.3	1,216	197	16.2
Drugs	4,892	137	2.8	5,849	429	7.3
Property	22,066	1,655	7.5	18,902	1,459	7.7
Total	**58,260**	**2,913**	**5.0**	**57,344**	**3,483**	**6.0**

1. Police files opened against suspects.

The fact that Israel provides crime opportunities for Palestinians is demonstrated by some of the figures taken from a victimization survey of Palestinian households in the West Bank and Gaza Strip. The crime rates in these areas are much lower than the rates attributed to Palestinians within Israel. Out of the 7,087 households surveyed, 1.8 percent had been victims of car theft, and 1.6 percent of larceny (excluding vehicular theft) (Palestinian Central Bureau of Statistics, 1996).

Relations between Israelis and Palestinians changed dramatically in December 1987 with the outbreak of the Palestinian Intifada. The uprising, which started as a series of confrontations between Israeli soldiers and crowds of angry and frustrated Palestinians, quickly escalated into a full-scale civil rebellion. This revolt bore little resemblance to any of the previous violent outbursts that had erupted from time to time since 1967 as part of the opposition and resistance to the occupation. Now, Israeli vehicles in Judea, Samaria, and the Gaza Strip were attacked by rocks and Molotov cocktails. These acts of belligerence led to frequent curfews and closures in all or parts of the territories, and the imposition of restrictions on entry into Israel. Thus, during the years of the Intifada, overall fewer Palestinians entered Israel, either for employment (legitimate or illegitimate), or for illegal acts (criminal or terrorist).

Although the events leading up to the Intifada were attributed to a series of specific confrontations between the Palestinians and Israeli forces in the Gaza

Strip, the PLO and other confrontational organizations promptly adopted it as part of the struggle for Palestinian national liberation. The many violent events that took place during the period of the Intifada, including terrorist attacks inside Israel (bus-bombing, stabbing, etc.) reflected the hostility of the Palestinians towards the Israeli occupation and their frustration in the effort to further their national aspirations, as well as the growing influence of Moslem fundamentalist movements.

Under the circumstances, one would expect that Palestinian offenders would be treated more harshly by the Israeli criminal justice system. Stereotypes that Israelis might hold regarding Arabs, in general, and Palestinian Arabs, in particular, would lead one to postulate that Palestinians would be likely to suffer discrimination in the judicial process in Israel.

In this chapter, we deal with the Palestinians as a distinct national group. In the current analysis, we choose to ignore the crimes of Palestinians that are clearly politically motivated. For instance, security offenses were excluded from all analyses extending beyond univariate or bivariate description. We focus on conventional forms of criminality, thereby enabling comparison of Palestinians with Jews and Israeli Arabs apprehended for similar offenses. Bear in mind, however, that the distinction between conventional and security offenses is not always clear-cut. Indeed, there may be considerable crossover, and decisions regarding offenses that qualify as security offenses to be tried in the military court are sometimes quite problematic. For instance, when a homicide occurs and the perpetrator is a Palestinian, it is the assigned motive, not simply the act itself that will determine whether it was an act of terrorism or a "regular" criminal homicide.

As noted, all of the Palestinian files included in this study were for crimes committed within the borders of Israel. Criminal offenses committed by Palestinians in the occupied territories are tried according to the Jordanian Penal Code in local courts, and security-related offenses and terrorist acts committed by Palestinians in the occupied territories are tried in military courts, which operate under a different legal code. Both of these categories fall outside the scope of the current study.

There were 5,384[2] Palestinian files in our total sample during the period (1980–1992) covered by the study. This figure includes security offenses committed in Israel which, as already indicated, were excluded from our analysis following the preliminary, purely descriptive, stage. The relatively low number of Palestinian files in our sample is hardly surprising, because as already mentioned, they represent only apprehensions for offenses committed within Israel. The low number may also reflect the fact that the number of Palestinians and their movement in Israel is subject to control and restriction. Moreover, it is sometimes extremely difficult for the long arm of the law to stretch out into remote Palestinian villages in the West Bank or densely populated refugee camps in the Gaza Strip in order to reach suspects.

The figures in table 28 reflect the prevailing political situation in the region.

Prior to the outbreak of the Intifada, property crimes were the most frequent offense committed by Palestinians (58.8%), followed by public order offenses (15.7%), causing bodily harm (9.2%) and security offenses (4.9%). After the outbreak of the Intifada (1990–1992), while property crimes were still the most frequent offense among Palestinians (41.1%), security offenses became the second most frequent offense (22.2%). The number of security offenses multiplied almost ninefolds (from 90 to 788 offenses), which is a clear reflection of the change in the political mood among the Palestinians in the West Bank and Gaza.

Table 28
Distribution of Offenses Committed by Palestinian Arabs by Period

Offense	Total		Period 1		Period 6	
	N	%	*N*	%	*N*	%
Security	878	16.3	90	4.9	788	22.2
Public Order	733	13.6	288	15.7	445	12.5
Against Human Life	40	0.7	4	0.2	36	1.0
Bodily Harm	412	7.7	168	9.2	244	6.9
Sex	107	2.0	65	3.5	42	1.2
Vice	439	8.2	86	4.7	353	9.9
Property	2,538	47.1	1,077	58.8	1,461	41.1
Fraud and Economic Crime	237	4.4	55	3.0	182	5.1
Total	**5,384**	**100.0**	**1,833**	**100.0**	**3,551**	**100.0**

Furthermore, table 28 shows that during the period of the Intifada, there was an overall increase in the rate of Palestinian files. Apart from sex offenses, the increase is evident in all categories following the outbreak of the Intifada. Following property and security offenses, come public order offenses. This category includes a variety of offenses, such as: illegal assembly, rioting, and assaulting a police officer. Many of the offenses in this category are related to political opposition to the occupation. However, although such offenses have been committed by Palestinians ever since the 1967 Six-Day War, their number almost doubled after the outbreak of the Intifada.

The increase in security offenses and public order offenses was to be expected; the increase in violence calls for more careful examination. The increased involvement of Palestinians in crimes of violence may be a reflection of a general trend in the late 1980s, following the outbreak of the Intifada. New types of offense were added to the list, such as throwing Molotov cocktails, erecting roadblocks, and burning tires. Rock-throwing was reclassified as an offense against human life. Most of such acts were carried out by Palestinians inside the occupied territories and, therefore, they do not form part of our data set. However, some were committed by Palestinian Arabs within the borders of the state of Israel, and these are included in our analysis. Some of such cases took place in east Jerusalem, which was annexed by the state of Israel after the

1967 Six-Day War and therefore counts as Israeli territory.

Traditionally, a clear distinction is made between conventional criminality and politically motivated crime (e.g., terrorism). However, here we assume that the two are closely intertwined. It is therefore interesting and theoretically important to find out whether the nationality factor affects decision making in the criminal justice system. In other words, we are interested in whether nationality ("being a Palestinian") affects judicial decision making and, if so, to what extent.

MULIVARIATE ANALYSIS

File Closure

A series of logistic regressions was performed to determine the likelihood of file closure among Palestinians in comparison to that of Jews and Israeli Arabs. The comparison yielded a number of interesting results. The general model (table 29), indicates that in comparison to Jews, Palestinians have a lower chance of having a file closed (i.e., a higher chance of being prosecuted). It is not surprising that Palestinians with prior files (-0.396) or prior convictions (-0.034), as well as those who are younger and unmarried, have a higher chance of being prosecuted. However, interestingly, there was an increase in the file closure rate during the period 1990–1992 (period 6, 0.719) during the peak of the Intifada. Not less interesting is the fact that in all other offense categories (violent offenses, public order offenses, and property offenses), nationality (Palestinian Arab or Jew) does not significantly affect the file closure decision (table 29). This finding also holds true for all models examined in table 30, comparing Palestinian Arabs and Israeli Arabs, except for the public disorder category.

In the framework of the general model (see table 30), there is no significant difference between the two groups in the probability of standing trial: "being a Palestinian Arab" or "being an Israeli Arab" has no significant effect on the file closure decision. Prior files and prior convictions (but not prior prison sentence) do have a significant effect—prior files, in general, and prior convictions, in particular, reduce the probability of file closure. Here, too, file closure increased (i.e., prosecution likelihood decreased) in the 1990–1992 period. This finding will be discussed in greater depth later in this chapter.

Next stage, we performed logistic regression analyses with control for selected offense categories. On the whole, the results are consistent with those obtained for the general model. Three offense categories were selected: violent offenses (against human life and bodily harm, combined), public order offenses, and property offenses—representing the most serious and frequent offenses. In all models, for all offense categories, regardless of whether Palestinians are compared to Jews, or Palestinians to Israeli Arabs, the results show conclusively

Table 29
Parameter Estimates of Logistic Regression: File Closure—Palestinian Arabs vs. Jews

Variable	General Mode	Violence	Public Order	Property
Palestinians	-0.122*	N.S.	N.S.	N.S.
Prior Files	-0.396*	-0.414*	-0.296*	-0.406*
Age	0.016*	0.014*	0.015*	0.019*
Married	0.191*	0.251*	0.103**	0.244*
Prior Prison	N.S.	0.248*	N.S.	N.S.
Prior Conviction	-0.034*	-0.031**	-0.54*	-0.027*
Period 6	0.719*	0.560*	0.621*	0.656*
Intercept	-0.454	-0.376	-0.385	-0.549
-2 log L	63530.594	9209.653	14612.695	25761.526
X^2 /df	5643.7/ 7	623.5/ 7	944.7/ 7	2244.1/ 7

* p<=.001
** p <=.02

Table 30
Parameter Estimates of Logistic Regression: File Closure—Palestinian Arabs vs. Israeli Arabs

Variable	General Model	Violence	Public Order	Property
Palestinians	N.S.	N.S.	0.439*	N.S.
Prior File	-0.304*	-0.315*	-0.188*	-0.313*
Age	0.011*	0.017*	0.009***	0.014*
Married	0.176*	N.S.	0.230**	0.132**
Prior Prison	-0.207*	N.S.	N.S.	N.S.
Prior Conviction	-0.026*	N.S.	-0.043**	N.S.
Period 6	0.829*	0.496*	0.513*	0.789*
Intercept	-0.644	-0.510	-0.737	-0.574
-2 log L	22675.072	3583.072	5057.312	9823.385
	1443.8/ 7	137.3/ 7	162.6/ 7	621/ 7

*p<=.001
**p <=.02
***p<= .05

that the probability of file closure increases after the outbreak of the Intifada. As expected, prior criminal involvement (prior files and convictions) decreases the probability of file closure, irrespective of offense category, and "being married" and "being older" increases the chances of file closure. There is no significant difference in the file closure rate for violent and property offenses in the comparison between Palestinians and Israeli Arabs. However, there is a significant difference for public order offenses—from table 30 we see that

Palestinians have a higher file closure probability (.439) than Israeli Arabs.

In order to see who has the highest and lowest chance of file closure, we calculated the estimated probabilities for various profiles of Jews, Israeli Arabs, and Palestinians on the basis of the regression analyses presented in this chapter and the equations presented in chapter 3. Estimated probabilities were calculated only for those models in which the nationality variable was found to have a significant effect, thus enabling comparison by nationality. In the case of file closure, this comparison was enabled for the general model and the public order offense category only.

From table 31, we see that in comparison to Jews, across offense category and across all profiles, Palestinians have a lower chance of having their files closed. This holds for both the first period of our study (1980–1982) and the last (1990–1992). For example, an 18-year-old Jewish suspect with no prior files has a 68 percent chance of having his file closed, whereas his Palestinian counterpart has only a 43 percent chance. There is also a noticeable difference before and after the outbreak of the Intifada—overall, file closure increases during the 1990–1992 period; the file closure rate for Jews with no prior files increases from 68 percent in period 1, to 81 percent in period 6; and for Palestinians, from 43 percent in period 1, to 61 percent in period 6.

Table 31
Predicted Probability for File Closure—Jews vs. Palestinian Arabs

	Period 1		Period 6	
General Model	**Jews**	**Palestinians**	**Jews**	**Palestinians**
Young;[1] 3 prior files; 3 prior convictions	0.19	0.10	0.32	0.30
Young; no prior files; no prior convictions	0.68	0.43	0.81	0.61
Old;[2] unmarried; 3 prior files; 3 prior convictions	0.25	0.13	0.60	0.24
Old; married; no prior files; no prior convictions	0.59	0.56	0.75	0.73

1. The probability for "young" was calculated for 18 years old.
2. The probability for "old" was calculated for 40 years old.

The file closure rate of Palestinians and Israeli Arabs diverges when specific offense categories are examined. In general, file closure increases from the first period of the study (1980–1981) to the last period (1990–1992), both among the Palestinians and Israeli Arabs. However, Palestinians have a higher chance of having their files closed than Israeli Arabs. Table 32 shows that the estimated probability for a Palestinian with no prior convictions is 54 percent, compared to 43 percent for an Israeli Arab. This trend persists across all profiles, across age groups, and is not dependent on prior criminal history. Marital status also plays a role in file closure decisions, with married suspects standing a better chance of having their files closed (see tables 30 and 31). The general model shows that an unmarried Jewish suspect, forty years old, with three prior files, and three prior convictions, has a .25 chance of having his file closed, whereas his Palestinian counterpart has a .03 chance of file closure. Note that married suspects with similar profiles have a similar chance of having their files closed (Jews .59, Palestinians.56). Note also that the file closure rate is even higher during 1990–1992 (period 6) (see tables 31 and 32). Similar findings are obtained for offenses against public order (table 32). A forty-five-year-old Israeli Arab with no criminal history has a .28 chance of having his file closed if he is unmarried, compared to.48 if he is married (during the period 1980–1982). The effect of marital status on file closure is evident for Palestinian suspects, too—a Palestinian suspect with the same profile who is unmarried has a .38 chance of having his file closed, compared to .58 if he is married.

It is hardly surprising that Palestinians have an overall higher probability to stand trial (i.e., no file closure) as compared to Jews. However, it is hard to explain why Israeli Arabs have a higher probability to stand trial compared to Palestinians. Furthermore, we also need to explain the general increase in the file closure rate during 1990–1992 (period 6), even among Palestinians (despite the deterioration in the relations between Israel and the Palestinians due to the Intifada).

Table 32
Predicted Probability for File Closure—Palestinian Arabs vs. Israeli Arabs in Public Order Offenses

Public Order Offenses	Period 1		Period 6	
	Israeli Arabs	Palestinians	Israeli Arabs	Palestinians
Young;[1] married; no prior files; no prior convictions	0.43	0.54	0.64	0.73
Young; unmarried; 3 prior files; 1 prior conviction	0.25	0.34	0.43	0.54
Old;[2] married; no prior files; no prior convictions	0.48	0.58	0.67	0.76
Old; unmarried; 3 prior files; 1 prior conviction; not married	0.28	0.38	0.47	0.58

1. Young refers to age 25.
2. Old refers to age 45.

We have already shown that the upward trend in file closure is independent of either offense category or nationality. Normally, such an increase in file closure can be explained by two related processes. One, an increase in the size of the police force takes place, which leads to the second process—an increase in the reported crime rate as a result of the increased output of a larger police force. In reality, what happened in Israel was that following the outbreak of the Intifada, the absolute size of the Israeli police force increased, and also a large number of personnel were shifted from administrative duties to operations. According to the official police publications, since 1987 there has been a net increase in the number of new recruits over the number of retirees (Israel National Police, Annual, Report 1991, p. 42). However, according to the official statistics (Crime in Israel, A Statistical Report 1996) the crime rate did not show a dramatic increase following the growth of the police. Between 1986 and 1996, the general crime trend in Israel fluctuated between fifty-one and fifty-nine per one thousand population, which is hardly an alarming rate of increase if one realizes that the population in Israel has increased during that time by close to 30 percent.

Following the small increase in crime rates, the question remains as to where all the increased police operational capacity diverted. In fact, it was applied toward law enforcement; however, that was not dramatically reflected in the crime rate. The nature of offending during the Intifada is characterized by many incidents of riots and other public order offenses. This led to massive arrests, sometimes indiscriminately, and opening of files only to be closed once the event was more thoroughly investigated. Some of the files will be closed by the police, and others at the level of the district prosecutor. As a matter of fact, what we have here is an increase in the number of arrests without a parallel increase in the number of criminal incidents. We suggest that this is an occurrence typical to times of public unrest, as well as during times of escalating crime rates. Under such circumstances, the police, in seeking to promote an image of efficiency tend to (mistakenly) open many files on the basis of less than stringent standards, only to close them subsequently. Clearly, although crime control is important, there is a price to be paid for extreme zealousness in view of the need to comply with due process—hence the high rates of file closure.

FROM ARREST TO CONVICTION

Palestinians, Jews, and Israeli Arabs in the Criminal Justice System

Once the decision to prosecute has been made, the main question is whether Palestinians, due to their problematic status, have a greater chance of being convicted than Jews or Israeli Arabs. We have already seen that, in general, Palestinians have a greater chance of standing trial (lower chance of having their files closed) in comparison to Jews, although not necessarily in comparison to Israeli Arabs. It is likely that these differences in favor of Jewish suspects stem from the overrepresentation of Palestinians in security offenses, an offense category in which Jews are hardly represented. Examination of the estimated probability of being convicted reveals a number of interesting trends.

When the general model is employed, without controlling for any of the offense categories, we find that Palestinians have a lower chance of being convicted than Jews and Israeli Arabs. This trend is clearly shown in table 33 and table 35 where the parameter estimate for nationality (Palestinian) when compared to Jews is -0.127, and when compared to Israeli Arabs, it is -0.465. We then calculated the estimated probability of being convicted based on the regression analysis in tables 33 and 35. The results obtained for the general model (tables 34 and 36) show clearly that across all profiles, Palestinians have a lower estimated probability of being convicted than Jews and Israeli Arabs.

However, when specific offense categories are analyzed, a slightly different picture is obtained. In the case of violent offenses (against human life and bodily harm, combined), Palestinian defendants, irrespective of criminal history and marital status, have a higher probability of being convicted than Jewish defendants. This result holds true for both the early period of our study (1980–1982) and the later period (1990–1992). A similar trend is also revealed in public order offenses—for the various profiles selected, the estimated probability

Table 33
Parameter Estimates of Logistic Regression: Conviction—Jews vs. Palestinians

Variable	General Model	Violence	Public Order	Property
Palestinians	-0.127*	0.311**	N.S.	0.093***
Prior File	0.016*	0.120*	N.S.	0.052*
Age	0.002***	N.S.	-0.004**	0.012*
Married	0.284*	N.S.	0.217*	0.362*
Prior Prison	0.288*	-0.299**	0.226**	0.589*
Prior Conviction	0.067*	0.062	0.077*	0.066*
Period 6	0.459*	0.300*	0.342*	0.413*
Intercept	-1.535	-1.433	-1.167	-1.877
-2 log L	5860.723	8065.678	13309.690	23596.766
x^2/df	3269.7/ 7	144.4/ 7	531.7/ 7	2008.0/ 7

* p<=.001
** p <=.02
*** p<= .05

of being convicted is higher among Palestinians than among Jews in both the first and the last period of the study (table 34). It is perhaps not surprising that marital status and age do not affect the disposition of the most serious offenses. (Neither of these variables was significant in the regression model [table 33], and, therefore, they were excluded from our estimated probability calculations.) We also examined the probability of being convicted in other offense categories, such as property and public order offenses. Results shown in table 34 reveal that for the various selected profiles, Palestinians have a higher probability of being convicted than Jews, although the discrepancies are not always very large. For instance, a twenty-five-year-old Jewish defendant, charged for a property offense, with three prior files and three prison terms behind him, has an estimated conviction probability of .60, compared to .62 for a Palestinian defendant with a similar profile. When there is no criminal history at all, the

Table 34
Predicted Probability for Conviction by Period and Nationality: Jews vs. Palestinian Arabs

General Model	Period 1 Jews	Period 1 Palestinians	Period 6 Jews	Period 6 Palestinians
Old; married; 3 prior files; 3 prior convictions; 1 prior prison	0.35	0.32	0.46	0.42
Young;[1] unmarried; no prior files; no prior prison	0.20	0.18	0.28	0.26
Old;[2] unmarried; no prior files; no prior prison	0.19	0.17	0.27	0.25
Married; 3 prior convictions; 1 prior prison	0.43	0.32	0.59	0.47
Married; no prior conviction; no prior prison	0.33	0.24	0.49	0.37
Unmarried; no prior convictions; no prior prison	0.27	0.19	0.41	0.31

1. Young refers to age18.
2. Old refers to age 40.

Violence	Period 1 Jews	Period 1 Palestinians	Period 6 Jews	Period 6 Palestinians
3 prior files; 3 prior prison	0.19	0.24	0.24	0.30
No prior files; no prior prison	0.12	0.16	0.16	0.20
Property Offenses				
Young; married; 3 pr files; 3 prior conviction; 3 prior prison.	0.60	0.62	0.70	0.72
Old; married; 3 pr files; 3 prior convictions; 3 prior prison	0.54	0.57	0.64	0.66
Young, unmarried; no prior files	0.20	0.22	0.28	0.30
Old, unmarried; no prior files	0.17	0.18	0.24	0.25
Public Order				
Young;[1] married; 3 prior files; 1 prior conviction	0.43	0.54	0.64	0.73
Young; unmarried; no prior files; no prior convictions	0.25	0.34	0.43	0.54
Old;[2] married; 3 prior files; 1 prior conviction	0.48	0.58	0.67	0.76
Old; unmarried; no prior files; no prior convictions	0.28	0.38	0.47	0.58

1. Young refers to age 25.
2. Old refers to age 45.

estimated probability of conviction for a property offense is .20 for a Jewish defendant and .22 for his Palestinian counterpart. As already mentioned in chapter 4, it is disturbing to find that criminal history plays a role in conviction, even though such information should not be available to the court prior to conviction, and therefore should not have an effect on the decision to convict. For instance, in public order offenses, a twenty-five-year-old defendant who has three prior files, among them one prior conviction, faces an estimated probability to be convicted of .43 if he is Jewish and .54 if he is a Palestinian. If there are no prior files, the probability drops to .25 for the Jewish defendant and .34 for the Palestinian. This pattern repeats itself for different age groups and offense categories. Careful examination of the differences between the first and last periods of the study also reveals an increase in the likelihood of conviction among both Jews and Palestinians.

Our next step was to compare the estimated probability of being convicted of Palestinians and Israeli Arabs. The picture obtained is not consistent with some of the earlier findings. The results of the regression analysis presented in table 36 clearly show that Israeli Arabs have a higher chance of being convicted than Palestinians. This holds true for the general model, as well as for the models analyzing violent offenses, public order offenses, and property offenses. We then calculated the estimated probabilities for various selected profiles of Palestinians and Israeli Arabs, as shown in table 36. Examination of the general model shows that, without exception, Palestinians have a lower chance of being convicted than Israeli Arabs. The findings for the specific offense categories presented in table 35 are inconsistent. For property offenses, we see that during the 1980–1982 period, Palestinians on trial for a property offense have a higher chance of being convicted than Israeli Arabs. The discrepancies during 1990–1992 (period 6) are not large and their direction is inconsistent—a twenty-five-year-old Palestinian, married, with three prior convictions and three prior prison sentences, has a .90 chance of being convicted, compared to .91 for his Israeli Arab counterpart. An opposite trend is obtained for defendants with no prior criminal history—for example, a twenty-five-year-old Palestinian with no prior file has a .29 chance of conviction compared to a .18 chance for his Israeli Arab counterpart.

There is a discrepancy in the estimated probability of conviction of Israeli Arabs and Palestinians who have prior files, but still, a twenty-five-year-old and forty-five-year-old Palestinian charged with a property offense faces a higher chance of being convicted than an Israeli Arab with the same profile, irrespective of criminal history. For public order offenses, Israeli Arabs stand a higher chance of being convicted than Palestinian defendants for all profiles (table 36).

Doing Time

Finally, after being convicted, the court will arrive at a sentencing decision: some will go to prison, some will be fined, and some will receive a suspended

Table 35
Parameter Estimates of Logistic Regression: Conviction—Israeli Arabs vs. Palestinian Arabs

Variable	General Model	Violence	Public Order	Property
Palestinians	-0.465*	N.S.	-0.429*	-0.290*
Prior File	N.S.	N.S.	N.S.	N.S.
Age	N.S.	N.S.	N.S.	0.012*
Married	0.300*	0.348*	0.357*	0.237*
Prior Prison	0.242*	N.S.	N.S.	0.433*
Prior Conviction	0.058*	N.S.	0.083*	0.056*
Period 6	0.657*	0.873*	0.727*	0.362
Intercept	-1.012	-1.191	-0.954	-1.274
-2 log L	22264.553	3297.285	4922.9220	9716.57
X^2/df	1065.6/ 7	135.9/ 7	185.3/ 7	475.5/ 7

* p<=.001

Table 36
Predicted Probability for Conviction by Period and Nationality: Palestinian Arabs vs. Israeli Arabs

	Period 1		Period 6	
General Model	**Israeli Arabs**	**Palestinians**	**Israeli Arabs**	**Palestinians**
Married; 3 prior convictions; 3 prior prison	0.60	0.50	0.75	0.62
Young;[1] unmarried; no prior files; no prior prison	0.20	0.18	0.28	0.26
Unmarried; no prior convictions; no prior prison	0.27	0.19	0.41	0.30
Property Offenses				
Young; married; 3 prior convictions; 3 prior prison	0.80	0.84	0.91	0.90
Old;[2] married; 3 prior convictions; 3 prior prison	0.83	0.88	0.93	0.91
Young	0.17	0.22	0.18	0.29
Old	0.21	0.27	0.22	0.34
Public Order				
Married; no prior convictions	0.35	0.26	0.53	0.42
Unmarried; 3 prior convictions	0.33	0.24	0.50	0.40

1. Young refers to age 25.
2. Old refers to age 45.

prison sentence. In this study, we focus on the extent to which, if at all, nationality (being a Jew, Israeli Arab, or Palestinian) affects the likelihood of receiving a prison sentence. We postulated that Palestinians (due to their high involvement in security offenses) will be more likely to receive a prison sentence. To date, no study has focused on Palestinians who commit offenses within the borders of the state of Israel. Statistics published by the Israel Prison Service are very general and provide no breakdown for offenses committed in Israel or the occupied territories. In 1986, out of a total of 8,748 inmates in Israeli prison facilities, 3,914 (44.7%) were Palestinians from the occupied territories. In 1995, the proportion of Palestinian inmates in Israeli prisons (including those detained for security offenses) went down to 22.5 percent (1,787 Palestinian inmates out of a total of 7,909) (Israel Prison Service, 1996). These figures provide no clue as to the likelihood of Palestinian offenders receiving a prison sentence.

We therefore examined the estimated probability of Palestinians receiving a prison term, compared to Jews and Israeli Arabs. In general, our findings indicate that the disparities between Jews and Palestinians are not large. The results obtained for the general model presented in table 38 (based on the regression analysis presented in table 37) reveal only marginal differences. For instance, when a forty-five-year-old offender, unmarried, with three prior files, one prior conviction, and one prior prison term is convicted again, the estimated likelihood of receiving a prison term is .80 if he is a Jew, compared to .87 in the case of a Palestinian. If he is married, the estimated likelihood of a prison term becomes .68 for a Jew and .80 for a Palestinian. A similar picture is obtained in relation to the property offense category, albeit with somewhat larger discrepancies—for example, the likelihood of a prison sentence for a first conviction is .04 for a Jew, and .09 for a Palestinian. A dramatic increase is observed when there is a prior criminal history. With three prior files, including one prior conviction, and one prior prison term, a Jewish offender has a .87 chance of receiving a prison sentence, compared to .94 for a Palestinian offender (table 38).

Table 37
Logistic Regression for Dependent Variable: Prison Sentence—Jews vs. Palestinian Arabs

Variable	General Model	Property
Palestinians	-2.828*	0.905*
Prior File	0.139*	0.205*
Age	-0.009*	N.S.
Married	-0.534*	-0.614*
Prior Prison	3.307*	3.827*
Prior Conviction	0.028*	0.031*
Period 6	N.S.	N.S.
Intercept	-2.828	-1.274
-2 log L	17,800	7965
X^2/df	1065.6/ 7	475.5/ 7

* p<=.001

Table 38
Predicted Probability for Receiving a Prison Sentence: Palestinian Arabs vs. Jews

General Model	Palestinians	Jews
Young;[1] married; male	0.08	0.045
Young; unmarried	0.15	0.09
Young; unmarried; 3 prior files; 1 prior conviction; 1 prior prison	0.88	0.81
Old;[2] married	0.07	0.04
Old; unmarried	0.13	0.08
Old; unmarried; 3 prior files; 1 prior conviction; 1 prior prison	0.87	0.80
Old; married; 3 prior files; 1 prior conviction; 1 prior prison	0.80	0.68
Property Offenses		
Married; no prior files; no prior convictions; no prior prison	0.09	0.04
Married; 3 prior files; 1 prior conviction; 1 prior prison	0.90	0.78
Unmarried; 3 prior files; 1 prior conviction; 1 prior prison	0.94	0.87

1. Young refers to age 25.
2. Old refers to age 45.

Finally, we compared the relative likelihood of Palestinians and Israeli Arabs to receive a prison sentence. This comparison was possible only for violent offenses (see table 39), because neither the variable representing nationality (Palestinian) nor the variables representing the time periods reached the required .05 level of significance in the regression models for other offense categories.

Although this model relates only to violent offenses, it is clear from the findings that when no prior criminal history is involved, the estimated probability of receiving a prison term is fairly low. The findings presented in table 40 show that a young Palestinian (unmarried) with no prior criminal history has a .04 probability of receiving a prison sentence, compared to .06 for an Israeli Arab convicted for a similar offense and with the same profile. No significant changes are observed during the later (1990–1992) period. A convicted Palestinian has a .02 probability of being sentenced to prison, and his Israeli Arab counterpart .03. The findings of the regression analysis indicate that the variable "prior prison sentence" has the strongest effect on the estimated likelihood of receiving a prison sentence. The results change significantly when there is a prior criminal history. A twenty-five-year-old (married) Palestinian with one prior prison sentence, has a .27 chance of receiving a prison term for the current conviction, compared to .40 for a convicted Israeli Arab. Marital status, as can be seen from table 39, also has an affect on the likelihood of receiving a prison sentence. A twenty-five-year-old, unmarried Palestinian with one prior prison term has a .45 probability of receiving a prison term in the current sentence, and an Israeli Arab with the same profile has an even higher (.60) probability.

Table 39
Logistic Regression for Dependent Variable: Prison Sentence for Palestinian Arabs vs. Israeli Arabs—Violent Offenses

Variable	Parameter Estimate	Pr > Chi-Square
Intercept	1.774	0.05
Palestinians	-0.547	0.05
Prior Files	-0.120	N.S.
Age	-0.149	0.001
Family Status	-0.777	0.0006
Prior Prison	2.308	0.0001
Prior Conviction	0.053	N.S.
Gender	0.883	N.S.
Period 2	-0.516	0.001
Period 3	-2.116	0.001
Period 4	-1.004	0.004
Period 5	-0.287	N.S.
Period 6	-0.773	0.0016
-2 log L	938.823	0.0001
X^2/df	287/12	

Table 40
Predicted Probability of Receiving a Prison Sentence by Nationality and Period for Palestinian Arabs vs. Israeli Arabs

	Period 1		Period 6	
Violent Offenses	**Israeli Arabs**	**Palestinians**	**Israeli Arabs**	**Palestinians**
Young; married; no prior prison	0.06	0.04	0.03	0.02
Young; unmarried; no prior prison	0.12	0.08	0.07	0.04
Young;[1] married; 1 prior prison	0.40	0.27	0.25	0.16
Young; unmarried; 1 prior prison	0.60	0.45	0.42	0.29
Old;[2] married; no prior prison	0.03	0.02	0.002	0.0009
Old; unmarried; no prior prison	0.007	0.004	0.004	0.002
Old; married; 1 prior prison	0.04	0.02	0.02	0.01
Old; unmarried; 1 prior prison	0.38	0.26	0.18	0.27

1. Young refers to age 25.
2. Old refers to age 45.

Two models examined the effect of specific offenses categories. Table 41 presents the model analyzed for property and public order offenses. In both offense categories, only Palestinians and Israeli Arabs could be compared, because the variables representing the period did not reach statistical significance. The findings are inconsistent; for property offenses, the probability of a Palestinian being sent to prison is greater than that of an Israeli Arab, with or without prior criminal files. The opposite trend is revealed in the case of public order offenses, were the estimated likelihood of a prison sentence is higher among Israeli Arabs than Palestinians across all four profiles presented in table 41.

While nationality had a clear effect on receiving a prison sentence (tables 38 to 41), in violent offenses, as well as property and public order offenses, we wanted to see whether length of imprisonment is also affected by any of these variables. An Ordinary Least Square regression analysis was employed in order to compare the effect of the independent variables on length of imprisonment among subjects from the three national groups (Jews, Israeli Arabs, and Palestinians). Nationality was found not to be statistically significant in predicting length of imprisonment (the table for this regression analysis is not presented here since the variables nationality was found not significant). The single most significant variable to predict the length of prison sentence is the number of prior prison sentences served, which is clearly a legal variable that might relate to the nature and dangerousness of the offender, an argument that clearly cannot be made in those instances in which nationality seem to have a determining affect on the legal fate of suspect or a defendant.

Table 41
Predicted Probability of Receiving a Prison Sentence by Nationality for Palestinian Arabs vs. Israeli Arabs in Property Offenses and Public Order Offenses

Property Offenses	Palestinians	Israeli Arabs
Married; no prior files	0.34	0.02
Unmarried; no prior files	0.02	0.01
Married; 1 prior file; 1 prior prison	0.69	0.55
Unmarried; 1 prior file; 1 prior prison	0.76	0.65
Public Order		
Married; no prior files	0.04	0.07
Unmarried; no prior files	0.09	0.16
Married; 1 prior file; 1 prior prison	0.38	0.55
Unmarried; 1 prior file; 1 prior prison	0.61	0.76

DISCUSSION

The Palestinian problem created by the establishment of the state of Israel created a unique situation that not only has political, but also social and legal implications. While the Palestinian problem had its political ramifications in the relations between Israel and its neighboring countries until 1967, its social, legal, and economic consequences were mostly pertinent to the Israeli Arabs. Only following the Six-Day War, with the occupation of the West Bank and the Gaza Strip, did Palestinian Arabs come into close contact, as individuals, with the Israeli society and its legal system. The economic ties, and the need of Palestinians to seek work in Israel, made them also prone as other residents to crime and legal sanctions. The stereotypes that might have affected the treatment of Israeli Arabs by the Israeli criminal justice system certainly should have also played a role also in the way Palestinians are treated by the Israeli criminal justice system.

The offenses we focused on were only those committed within the recognized borders of Israel, and those which are really comparable offenses. In other words, we did not examine and compare the response of the Israeli system to security offenses that are very rare among Israelis which when committed by Palestinians evoke other emotions besides the need to do justice.

From the onset of the study, our hypothesis was that Palestinians would have the lowest rate of file closure (which means a higher chance of standing trial) than Jews and Israeli Arabs when controlling for type of offense. Furthermore, that the conviction rate for Palestinians would be the highest, as would be the chance to receive a prison sentence. We also expected to find that the length of the sentence for Palestinians would be the longest, compared to Jews and Israeli Arabs.

The data very accurately reflects the effect political events had on criminal behavior. Following the 1967 occupation and prior to the Intifada security offenses were very scarce within the borders of Israel (about 4% to 5% of all Palestinian offenses), but it changed dramatically following the outbreak of the Intifada and was the second most prevalent offense (over 22% of all offenses committed by Palestinians).

When compared to Jews, the results are consistent with the hypotheses. Palestinians, overall, have a greater chance to stand trial. However, when compared on specific offense categories—violent offenses, public order offenses, and property offenses—the nationality variable is not found to make a significant difference. This must lead one to assume that the security offenses, unique to the Palestinians, are those that affect the results of the general model (which does not differentiate between offense categories). When Israeli Arab and Palestinian file closure are compared, it appears from the general model that nationality does not affect file closure, with one exception. Palestinians have a higher rate of file closure than Israeli Arabs in the case of public order offenses. This unexpected result cannot be because of greater tolerance toward Palestinians than toward Israeli Arabs, but it may suggest that during incidents classified as public order offenses, more innocent Palestinian bystanders are detained and quickly released following a more thorough investigation of the events.

The results also show that as has been the case with Jews and Arabs (see chapter 4) as well as Palestinians, the tendency to close files of suspects has dramatically increased at the last period, and is consistent across offenses and offender profiles.

The pattern of conviction seems to be contradicting the hypotheses. Both Jews, and even more so, Israeli Arabs have a higher probability of conviction than Palestinians when the logistic regression model does not specify the offense category (general model). This finding is consistent across ages and criminal histories. However, the findings do not persist when specific offenses are controlled for. Thus, in crimes against person and against public order, Palestinians have a higher chance than Jews of being convicted in all possible profile combinations of age, marital status, and criminal history. In the case of property offenses, the pattern is mixed and there are profiles in which Jews have a higher probability of conviction than Palestinians. This should lead one to assume that in property offenses the nationality does not seem to play a role as far as convictions are concerned, while the systematic higher chance of Palestinians being convicted in crimes against person and public order offenses might indicate a bias or discrepancy.

Israeli Arabs have a higher chance of being convicted when compared to Palestinians. This is a consistent pattern according to the general model (when offense categories are not controlled for), as well as when examining specific crime categories. This leads one to suspect, again due to the consistency of the pattern across different offense categories and offender profiles, that Israeli Arabs are treated more punitively than Palestinians by the courts.

Here, one should be aware of the continuous pattern of increased conviction probabilities for all groups in the last period, which seems contradictory to the pattern of file closure, which is on the increase for the same time period.

Finally, when examining the probability of receiving a prison sentence, it seems that, overall, the differences which exist between Palestinians and Jews are very small, but nevertheless consistent. It should be noted that when criminal history exists, the probability of receiving a prison sentence increases very dramatically for Jews and Palestinians alike. These results do show discrepancy, but if a systematic and intentional, conscious, discrimination is the norm, the differences should have been much higher.

As far as the comparison between Israeli Arabs and Palestinians is concerned, the only significant difference is detected in violent offenses, where the Israeli Arabs, controlling for everything else, are treated more punitively by the system, and have a higher probability of getting a prison sentence.

It is interesting to note that the length of imprisonment is totally unaffected by nationality, and the best single predictor of length of one's prison sentence is the number of prior prison sentences served.

In the last chapter of this book, we will discuss the existence and extent of discrimination by nationality in Israel's criminal justice system in greater detail, and analyze how political events over the ten-year period covered by our study affected judicial decision making.

NOTES

1. The victory of the Israeli defense forces over three Arab countries in six days symbolized, for many Jews all over the world, the independent capability of Israel to

defend itself against its enemies. This, and what turned out to be more than thirty years of occupation, was perceived as glorious military operation. As a result, the image of the state of Israel changed and a large wave of immigration, especially from Western Europe and North America, followed during the years immediately thereafter.

2. The discrepancy between this figure and the figure in table 2 in chapter 3, is due to records that have been deleted from the multivariate analysis in this chapter, because of too many missing variables.

7

Perceived Injustice as Legitimation for Illegal Behavior

To date, there has been no large-scale, empirical study of how Arabs in Israel relate to the law and the criminal justice system, and whether their attitudes and perceptions are constructed differently than those of their Jewish counterparts. A number of studies have assumed that due to legislation such as: the Law of Return (which provides automatic citizenship for Jewish immigrants); statutes that grant privileges to those who have completed their military service (which discriminate against Arabs because they are exempt from conscription); and statutes that grant preferential treatment to Jewish citizens in areas such education, public housing, health, and employment, there exists a residue of perceived injustice among Israeli Arabs (Kretzmer 1990; Peretz 1988). In this chapter, we report the findings of a survey attempting to examine whether the differential treatment of Israeli Arabs reported in our study has left its mark on the attitudes and perceptions of Israeli Arabs towards the criminal justice system. In addition, we examine whether any such built-up sense of injustice leads to delegitimation of the law and Israel's legal institutions and, if so, whether those who challenge the legitimacy of the Israeli law also consider themselves free to violate it, or "take the law into their own hands."

During the past decade, social scientists have expressed growing interest in the relationship between compliance with the law and factors such as prejudice, injustice, race, ethnicity, mistrust, and discriminatory practices (Biafora et al. 1993; Tyler 1990; Taylor et al. 1994; George-Abeyie 1984; Terrell 1980; Terrell, Terrell and Taylor 1981). Although some of the studies have remained speculative, others represent a serious empirical effort towards arriving at a better understanding of the relationships between legal compliance and other social factors. For instance, Taylor et al. (1994), using survey data from Miami, Florida, tested whether racial mistrust is related to the willingness of African American, Haitian, and other Caribbean Island, black adolescent boys to engage in delinquent behaviors. The main hypothesis guiding this study was that racial mistrust may encourage both dissatisfaction with the law and a disposition towards deviance that runs counter to law-abiding expectations. The findings show that compared to white non-Hispanics, African American and Haitian blacks are more ready to violate the law, and that such conduct has certain rewards. The findings also suggest that adolescents with a lower socioeconomic background are more likely to view lawbreaking as acceptable, and perhaps even desirable. It was found that Haitians often expressed anger at the legal system in that it was perceived as treating them differently from individuals of other national and racial origin. Their perception of anti-Haitian discrimination is further compounded by their triple social marginality—they are black, speak a foreign language, and their culture is at variance with both the dominant white culture and the local black culture. However, these findings are not generalizable beyond the south Florida area due to the uniqueness of the immigrant community in this region.

Based on the experience of previous studies and our knowledge and understanding of Israeli society, we assumed that when injustice is both experienced and perceived as such by various individuals or members of groups in society, it may lead to some degree of delegitimation of the law and the legal system, and even readiness to disobey it, or take the law into one's own hands. On the basis of this assumption, we hypothesized that in a divided society such as Israel:

(a) there would be a general link between socioeconomic status and perceived injustice or, more specifically, that lower socioeconomic status would be associated with a higher level of perceived injustice;

(b) the above link would be related to more readiness to take the law into one's own hands or, more specifically, the stronger the sense of injustice, the greater the tendency to take the law into one's own hands;

(c) Arabs, as members of an ethnic minority group as well as an economically underprivileged sector of Israeli society, would express a greater sense of injustice and be more ready to violate the law or to take it into their own hands.

DATA AND METHODS

The Sample

The above hypotheses were tested by conducting a specially designed, large-scale survey. Due to the different socioeconomic and demographic structures of the Jewish and Arab communities in Israel, the two groups were sampled separately. A single random sample would not have yielded the 18 percent representation of Arabs in the total population, and would have been too small to allow for adequate representation of the various subgroups within the Arab population (rural, urban, etc.), as well as for multivariate analysis.

Using a list of all of the telephone area codes, subjects were randomly selected from each area relative to the proportion of the area's population in the whole country. This procedure guaranteed proportional representation of populations in rural and remote areas which, by a simple random sampling procedure, might not have been represented at all, and was especially helpful in obtaining proper representation of the Arab population. This procedure yielded two random samples consisting of 901 Jews and 965 Arabs, 1,866 subjects in all.

After selection of households, standard procedures were used to select respondents randomly. The interviews were conducted by telephone, in Hebrew or Arabic, depending on the respondent's language, and lasting fifteen to twenty minutes each. The telephone interview method of data collection was selected because it is inexpensive and, in view of the subject matter, was believed to yield more reliable results.

The Jewish sample was composed of 59 percent females and 41 percent males and the Arab sample, 48 percent females and 52 percent males. The age structure of both samples was quite similar, with median age of thirty five in the Jewish sample and thirty in the Arab sample. About 11 percent of the Jewish respondents and 5 percent of the Arab respondents were above the age of sixty five. The educational level of the Jewish respondents was higher than that of the Arab respondents: higher (postsecondary) education, Jews 38 percent, Arabs 23 percent; full secondary school education, Jews 50 percent, Arabs 29 percent; and less than full high school education, Jews 12 percent, Arabs 48 percent.

Research Instrument

The questionnaire constructed for the survey is presented in table 42 (together with the percentage distribution of the responses on all items). Two versions, one in Hebrew and one in Arabic, were used. All questionnaire items (Q1–Q20) had a Likert-type response scale of 1 to 5 (1 indicating absolute disagreement and 5 indicating absolute agreement).

The questionnaire covered a range of issues, all related to the law and the legal system. Items Q1 Q2, Q6 and Q13-Q18 deal with the obligation to obey the law, both in general and under special circumstances. A series of items, Q3, Q4, Q5, Q7, Q19, and Q20 deal with perceived discrimination by the law and its agencies (the police, court, etc.). The remainder deal with other general issues related to the criminal justice system, such as the conviction of innocent people, the use of force by the police, and disproportionate punishment. In addition, we operationalized the following socioeconomic variables:

(a) education: 1 = incomplete secondary school; 2 = complete secondary school; 3 = higher education.

(b) income: 1 = monthly income of 2,000 N.I.S or less; 2 = 2,001-3,000 N.I.S; 3 = 3,001-4,000 N.I.S; 4 = 4,001-5,000 N.I.S; 5 = 5,001-6,000 N.I.S; 6 = 6,000 or more (where 1 N.I.S = 3.7 U.S dollars, April 1998).

Table 42
Percentage of Jews and Arabs Responding to Survey

		Jews						Arabs					
		1	2	3	4	5	Total	1	2	3	4	5	Total
Q1.	A citizen in the state of Israel has to obey all laws without exception	7	8	5	29	51	100%	3	17	1	37	42	100%
Q2.	A citizen in the state of Israel has to obey only those laws that seem reasonable to him	39	29	4	14	14	100%	5	35	1	36	23	100%
Q3.	Court decisions are usually fair	9	22	14	36	19	100%	5	42	6	37	10	100%
Q4.	Laws in Israel are often unjust and discriminatory	17	25	13	30	15	100%	5	24	7	46	18	100%
Q5.	The courts in Israel discriminate against Arabs	35	28	20	11	6	100%	8	29	8	37	17	100%
Q6.	Violating the law is not terrible, as long as one does not get caught by the police	59	24	4	8	5	100%	41	44	3	9	3	100%
Q7.	Police conduct is discriminatory	22	25	18	23	12	100%	8	27	7	41	17	100%
Q8.	When the law and its representatives (i.e., police) cannot protect the citizens, citizens can take the law into their own hands	50	29	5	11	5	100%	14	31	4	39	12	100%
Q9.	The chances of an innocent person being convicted in court are very small	12	21	15	35	17	100%	4	25	8	52	12	100%
Q10.	Violators of the law are caught and punished very often	22	33	15	21	10	100%	12	38	3	37	10	100%

1=absolutely disagree
5=absolutely agree

		Jews						Arabs					
		1	2	3	4	5	Total	1	2	3	4	5	Total
Q11.	Punishments imposed by the courts in Israel are not proportionate to the severity of the offense	13	19	18	33	17	100%	5	37	10	40	8	100%
Q12.	Police can use exaggerated force to fulfill its duties	47	25	7	14	8	100%	20	45	3	28	5	100%
Q13.	When the law conflicts with my own interests, I have the right to disobey the law	41	36	8	10	5	100%	32	37	5	18	8	100%
Q14.	I am ready to accept punishment for violating a law that conflicts with my interests	15	16	6	25	38	100%	3	17	3	59	19	100%
Q15.	I am not ready to violate a law that conflicts with my interests, but I am ready to tolerate other people doing so	50	24	8	11	6	100%	22	50	5	22	1	100%
Q16.	As a citizen, I have the right to disobey a law on ideological grounds	37	36	10	12	5	100%	24	33	10	23	10	100%
Q17.	I am ready to accept a punishment for disobeying a law on ideological grounds	17	12	9	31	31	100%	2	15	2	62	18	100%
Q18.	I am ready to tolerate other people disobeying a law on ideological grounds	49	26	7	12	6	100%	3	47	7	22	2	100%
Q19.	The legal system is very lenient towards people who violate a law on ideological grounds	16	26	22	22	13	100%	12	39	17	30	2	100%
Q20.	Laws in Israel serve all citizens equally, and not specific groups	12	17	13	37	21	100%	11	37	6	38	8	100%

Data Analysis

The analysis of the data was carried out in two stages. In the first, descriptive stage, the frequency distributions of the Jewish and Arab responses to the questionnaire items were mapped out. In the second stage, a multivariate analysis was carried out using LISREL-8 as the method of analysis.[1] Readiness to violate or take the law into one's own hands was defined as the dependent variable. The multivariate analysis examined how the various independent variables cluster together, and how each of these clusters affects the dependent variable. The clusters were determined by a factor analysis, and their reliability was measured by the Alpha-Cronbach coefficient. These clusters are referred to as latent variables by the LISREL procedure.

Two hypotheses were tested by the multivariate analysis:

(a) H_1—Socioeconomic status (SES) will be negatively associated with measures of perceived injustice among both Jews and Arabs or, more specifically, lower income and educational level will be associated with higher levels of perceived injustice.

(b) H_2—Measures of perceived injustice will be positively associated with lawbreaking or, more specifically, higher levels of perceived injustice will be associated with higher levels of readiness to violate or take the law into one's own hands.

RESULTS

Univariate Analysis

Jews and Arabs alike (80% and 79%, respectively) generally agreed with the statement that the law should be obeyed without exception (Q1). However, this finding is not consistent with the response to the item suggesting that a citizen has to obey only those laws that seem reasonable to him (Q2): 59 percent of the Arabs compared to 28 percent of the Jews, were inclined to agree with this statement. The next four questions (Q3–Q6) focused on issues related to the Israeli criminal justice system (the police, the courts, etc.). As many as 31 percent of the Jews and 47 percent of the Arabs disagreed with the statement that court decisions in Israel are usually fair. The sense of injustice among Arabs was found to be even stronger with regard to the laws themselves—some 64 percent of the Arabs, compared to about 45 percent of the Jews agreed with the statement that that laws in Israel are often unjust and discriminatory (Q4). Similarly, 48 percent of the Arabs (compared to 29 percent of the Jews) did not agree that laws in Israel serve all citizens equally (Q20). With regard to specific discrimination against Arabs (Q5), the sense of injustice was found to be much stronger among the Arabs—54 percent of the Arabs, compared to 17 percent of the Jews, agreed that the courts in Israel discriminate against them. When asked about police conduct (Q7), 58 percent of the Arabs, compared to 35 percent of the Jews, indicated that the police handling is discriminatory.

Several items dealt with disobedience and "taking the law into one's own hands." The findings show that 16 percent of the Jewish respondents agreed that they have the right to take the law into their own hands, whereas more than 50 percent of the Arabs agreed with such an option (Q8). Arabs (26%) more than Jews (15 %) tended to agree that they have the right to violate the law if and when it conflicts with their own interests (Q13). Another dimension of this latter question was willingness to tolerate such violations in others (Q15): 17 percent of the Jews and 23 percent of the Arabs responded in the affirmative on this item. Ideological justification of such disobedience (Q16) was found among 17 percent of the Jews compared to almost twice as many Arabs (33%). Of the 17 percent of the Jews who felt that they have the right to violate the law on ideological grounds, 62 percent were ready to accept punishment for such action, and an even higher proportion of the Arabs (80 percent) were willing to accept the consequences (Q17). When asked about willingness to tolerate such violations in others on ideological grounds, the numbers dropped to 18 percent among the Jews, and 24 percent among the Arabs.

In addition, several other questions were asked dealing with more general issues related to the criminal justice system. Most respondents agreed that the chances of an innocent person being convicted are low (Q9), but still 33 percent of the Jews and 29 percent of the Arabs did not agree with this statement. When asked about the efficiency of the system, only 45 percent of the Jews and 50 percent of the Arabs thought that offenders are often caught and punished (Q10). Another indication of how efficient the system is perceived is reflected by the finding that 50 percent of the Jews and 48 percent of the Arabs were of the opinion that punishments imposed by the courts in Israel are not proportional to the severity of the offense (Q11).

The results clearly suggest that the criminal justice system is not perceived as efficient. The apprehension rate is perceived to be low, and the punishments imposed on convicted offenders are not perceived to be proportional to the severity of the offense. On the normative level, the differences between Arabs and Jews are insignificant, with about 20 percent of the respondents of the opinion that it is the duty of a citizen to obey the law. Selective compliance with the law seems to be supported by a majority of Arabs (59%) and only 28 percent of the Jews. However, in both groups there is a disturbing feeling that the laws are discriminatory and unjust and, albeit to a lesser degree, that police handling is discriminatory (Arabs, 58%; Jews, over one-third). These results do not bode well for the Israeli justice system—the differences between Jews and Arabs are fairly consistent, but at the same time, the level of dissatisfaction, although very high among Arabs, is also quite disturbing among Jews. There is a clear erosion in the status of the law—the direction of this survey's casts strong doubts on commitment to the rule of law according to accepted definitions of modern democracy.

Multivariate Analysis

We tested our hypotheses using a multiple structural equation model designed to treat ordinal variables; namely, the LISREL-8 maximum likelihood method (Joreskog and Sorbom, 1993). Figure 7 gives the structural model initially hypothesized by us:

Figure 7
Hypothesized Structural Model

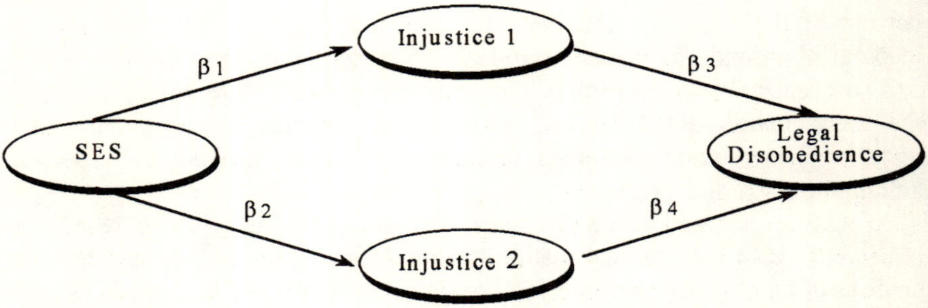

Table 43 presents the findings of the confirmatory factor analysis employed by LISREL, testing the construct validity of latent variables for the respective models for Jews and Arabs. The confirmatory factor analysis is referred to as the measurement model. For each construct, one regression weight λ on the latent variable was constrained to 1.0 for the purpose of the model identification. Thus, the latent variables were measured in the same units as the observed variables on which the regression weights were constrained. Table 43 shows that a significant amount of variance on the observed variables was accounted for by the constructed latent variables, thus validating the measurement of the theoretical construct.

Two structural models, one for the Jewish and the other for the Arab sample, were constructed. In both models, SES is measured by income and education level. Questionnaire items Q3 and Q5 together form a latent variable, measuring perceived injustice regarding court decisions (Injustice 1). This factor (latent variable) reflects general dissatisfaction with court decisions in both the Jewish and Arab samples. The standardized estimates on Q5 suggest that this variable has a somewhat stronger effect in the Arab sample than in the Jewish sample (.83 and .81, respectively). Questionnaire items Q4 and Q7 together form another factor (latent variable), measuring discrimination by the law and by the police (Injustice 2). The existence of this factor further substantiates the picture regarding perceived injustice among both Jews and Arabs.

Table 43
Maximum Likelihood Estimates of Construction Validity for Jewish and Arab Subjects

Parameter	Standardized Estimates	Unstandardized Estimates	S.E.	P <	Alpha Cronbach Coefficient
Jews					
SES					
Income	0.49	1.00	—		
Education	0.56	2.18	0.46	0.001	0.81
Injustice 1					
Q3	0.85	1.00	—		
Q5	0.81	0 .97	0.19	0.05	0.86
Injustice 2					
Q4	0.73	1.00	—		
Q7	0.69	2.65	1.20	0.05	0.91
Legal Disobedience					
Q1	-0.75	-1.00	—		
Q2	-0.69	-1.12	0.17	0.0001	
Q8	0.78	2.41	0.65	0.0001	
Q13	0.81	1.49	0.54	0.05	0.88
Arabs					
SES					
Income	0.18	1.00	—		
Education	0.12	0 .58	2.23	0.05	0.83
Injustice 1					
Q3	0.79	1.00	—		
Q5	0.83	1.74	0.19	0.05	0.89
Injustice 2					
Q4	0.80	1.00	—		
Q7	0.75	2.65	1.20	0.05	0.93
Legal Disobedience					
Q1	-0.56	-1.00	—		
Q2	-0.81	-1.12	0.17	0.0001	
Q8	0.18	2.41	0.65	0.0001	
Q13	0.77	1.49	0.54	0.05	
Q16	0.68	1.49	0.54	0.05	0.84

Several items related to lawbreaking and the perceived right to take the law into one's own hands together formed a "Legal Disobedience" factor. Among the Jewish respondents, this latent variable is formed by the observed variables Q1, Q2, Q8, and Q13, all of which deal with the hypothetical right of a citizen to disobey the law and take the law into his/her own hands. In the Arab sample, a fifth item, Q16, dealing with legal disobedience on ideological grounds, is also associated with this latent variable. This item did not reach statistical significance in the Jewish sample and, therefore, it was not included in model 1.

Figures 8 and 9 present the causal relationships between the latent variables SES, Injustice 1, Injustice 2, and the dependent variable, Legal Disobedience. All the parameter estimates in both models were significant at the .05 level, at least. Contrary to our hypothesis (H_1), the findings suggest that SES has a positive effect on perceived injustice—Higher SES Jewish respondents exhibit higher levels of perceived injustice than their lower SES counterparts on both Injustice 1 (β_1=.29) and Injustice 2 (β_2=.38). Traditionally, the literature suggests that injustice at the hands of the criminal justice system is experienced mainly by persons belonging to the lower socioeconomic sectors of society. Hence, one would also expect that they would also express a higher degree of dissatisfaction with criminal justice outcomes and that dissatisfaction expressed under such circumstances might be a direct reaction to their experience of injustice at the hands of the criminal justice system. It would therefore be understandable to find higher levels of perceived injustice among respondents of low SES. Our finding that the higher SES, the higher the level of dissatisfaction with the legal system, suggests that the feelings of injustice expressed by these

Figure 8
Path Diagram and Standardized Structural Coefficients for Jewish Subjects

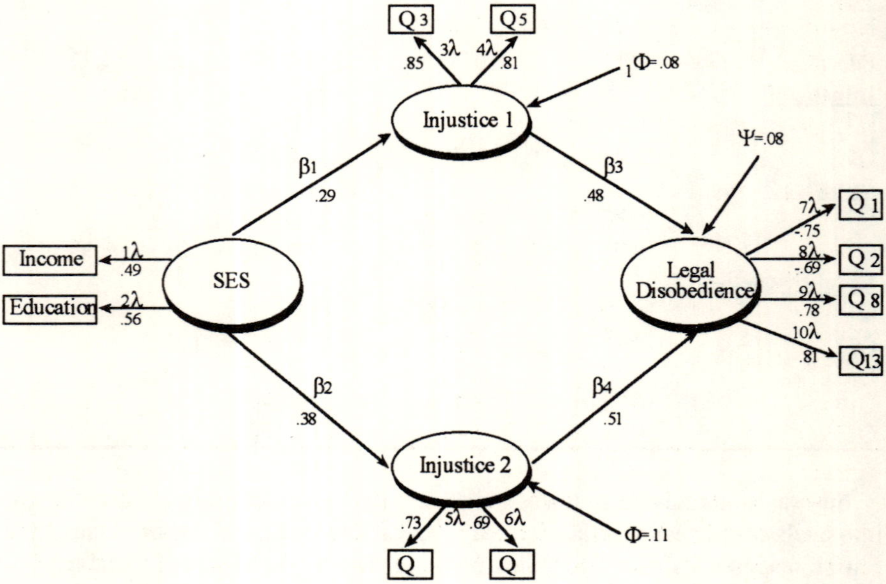

respondents, who are less likely to have experienced direct injustice, stem from a normative critical approach towards the system.

The model further indicates, as hypothesized, that both measures of injustice are positively associated with Legal Disobedience—Jewish respondents with stronger feelings of injustice expressed more readiness to take the law into their own hands (β_3=.48 and β_4=.51).

Figure 9 presents the findings for the Arab sample. Here, too, SES is positively associated with both Injustice 1 and Injustice 2. However, the standardized estimates β_1=.15 and β_2=.18 indicate that the association between SES and perceived injustice is weaker than in the Jewish model.

On the other hand, and in line with our hypothesis (H_2), both measures of injustice exhibit a stronger positive association with Legal Disobedience in the Arab model (β_3=.68 and β_4=.72).

Figure 9
Path Diagram and Standardized Structural Coefficients for Arab Subjects

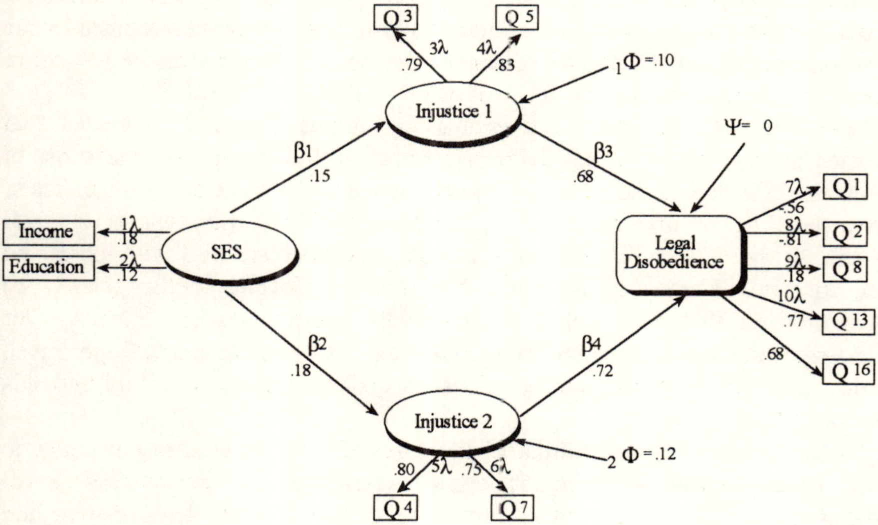

DISCUSSION

The above findings go beyond simply indicating how Jews and Arabs perceive the Israeli criminal justice system. The analysis enabled us to construct causal models that show how factors related to SES and perceived injustice are linked to one another, and how the overall model explains the phenomenon of "taking the law into one's own hands" among both Jews and Arabs.

One of the main findings of the data analysis is that 15 percent of the Jews in the sample and 20 percent of the Arabs did not see themselves bound by a *prima facie* obligation to obey the law under all circumstances. Ideological justification for legal disobedience among both Jews and Arabs is stated in terms of principles such as freedom, equality, and national independence. This is probably the main reason for the differences found between the response mode to the first and second questions (Q1, Q2). When asked in general terms about the need to obey the law, members of both groups overwhelmingly support compliance (80%). However, at the same time, 28 percent of the Jews and some 59 percent of the Arabs seem to hold the opinion that one needs to obey only those laws with which one agrees. This response mode probably indicates that the first question taps a general, normative, ethical response, whereas the second represents a response to specific laws considered to be unreasonable. It would be almost natural to assume that, in comparison to Jews, Arabs, as members of a minority group, would have to confront unjust legal situations (laws, court decisions, etc.) more frequently than Jews and, hence, their much stronger feelings regarding the right to disobey the law.

Indeed, the findings of this analysis confirm our assumption that Arabs, due to being a national minority, are more likely to suffer injustice and, therefore, exhibit stronger feelings of perceived injustice with regard to the penal code, the courts, and police conduct. This notion of injustice is further substantiated by the responses obtained to Q20: 48 percent of the Arabs, compared to 29 percent of the Jews, rejected the statement that laws serve all citizens equally.

According to the models presented in Figures 8 and 9, it seems that socioeconomic status is positively associated with both of our measures of injustice: the higher the SES, the higher the perceived level of injustice. These two measures of injustice, in turn, are associated with the concept of legal disobedience. Thus, the direction of the link between SES and perceived injustice runs counter to our initial hypothesis. Following conflict theory, we hypothesized that SES would be negatively associated with injustice. Our findings show that, on the contrary, SES is positively associated with perceived injustice regarding laws, court decisions, and police conduct. This finding holds for both Jews and Arabs.

It is plausible that the attitudinal measures of injustice used in our study do not reflect actual injustice as often experienced by persons of lower socioeconomic status, but rather normative criticism of the legal system and skepticism regarding the obligation to comply with the law. This latter mode tends to be observed among members of privileged groups who may not have actually experienced injustice. This type of mode can be interpreted as criticism of the system—a form of "legitimized illegalism."

In contrast to the Jews, Arabs tend to legitimize their readiness to violate the law in ideological terms. This finding may be due to the fact that Arabs, as a minority group, feel more compelled to justify and give "legitimate" reasons for their readiness to disobey the law. Among the Jews, justification of this type is more likely to be confined to ideological extremists and political zealots. However, due to their small number in the general Jewish population, the chance of their being represented in this or any other random sample is very slight.

Our findings shed light on some of the consequences of living as a minority group in Israel and, in particular, as clients of the criminal justice system. The feelings of injustice that stem from the very nature of Israeli laws and police conduct tend to induce feelings of discrimination among Arabs. Our exploration of the various junctures of the criminal justice system reveals clear discrepancies between the "amount of justice" enjoyed by Jews and Arabs. The probability of standing trial and being convicted is slightly higher for Arabs than Jews. Furthermore, once convicted, the likelihood of receiving a prison sentence is significantly higher among Arabs than among Jews. Among members of a national minority under such circumstances, over time, and even without feeling a sense of blatant discrimination (the differences are much smaller than originally anticipated), the feeling of marginality and lack of relevance of the system is likely to lead to distrust of the system, strong feelings of injustice, delegitimation of the legal system, and willingness (under certain conditions) to disobey the law.

NOTE

1. The LISREL analysis consists of two parts: the measurement of the model and the structural equation model. The measurement model specifies how latent variables or hypothetical constructs depend upon, or are indicated by, the observed variables. This procedure is similar to confirmatory factor analysis and attempts to test which of the variables cluster together. The structural equation model specifies the causal relationships among the latent variables and describes the causal effects.

8

The Rule of Law in Israeli Society: Conclusions

What is the meaning of "the rule of law"? According to former Deputy Chief Justice Haim Cohen (Gabison, 1987), under the rule of law: "a right cannot be breached unless by law: It is the prerogative of the law, and only of the law, to control or to deny a right." The stability of a democracy cannot be measured at one point of time—it has a longitudinal dimension. The basic requirements of democracy; namely, majority rule and compliance with basic norms, have to be seen to endure over time. Democracy in action represents a fragile balance between majority rule, on one hand, and the need to protect basic norms such as human rights, on the other (Chief Justice Barak 1986). Thus, in a free democracy, the written word of the law prescribes certainty, publicity, and, above all, equality. However, there is no guarantee that these components of the rule of law will always prevail over all other considerations. Law and justice, after all, are not carved out in stone. Judicial decisions are rendered not only on the basis of clear-cut rules, but also interpretation. Discretionary power, which lies at the basis of judicial behavior at all levels, impinges on the element of uniformity and may, therefore, lead to inequality in decision making. Indeed, it is the exercise of discretionary power at various junctures of the criminal justice system that is often responsible for setting guilty people free, on one hand, and convicting innocent people, on the other. In their book, *Convicted But Innocent: Wrongful Conviction and Public Policy*, Huff, Rattner, and Sagarin (1996) examine the stunning potential for error in the criminal justice system—the conviction of the innocent. Based on a comprehensive analysis of more than six hundred cases of wrongful conviction (many of them with no probable cause of guilt, but unfortunate enough to be identified with the margins of society), the authors document how various factors such as eyewitness identification, prosecutorial and police misconduct, inadequate legal representation, and coerced confession, contribute toward the conviction of innocent people.

Although some of the errors (e.g., eyewitness identification) result from mechanisms inherent in criminal procedure, other judicial errors were found to be closely related to cultural expectations formed by past experience, stereotyping, and personal prejudice. In their analysis, the authors show that although many convicted innocents in the United States are white, and some are also middle-class, a disproportionate number are black or Hispanic who were treated by prejudiced police officers, prosecutors, and even judges, and eventually convicted by an all-white jury. However, of all the errors described, the main factor in wrongful conviction was found in the discretionary power exercised by criminal justice officials (police officers, prosecutors, and judges) and applied unequally to members of various social groups.

Justice systems are often characterized as adhering either to the crime control model or the due process model (Packer 1968). The crime control model adopts the proposition that the repression of criminal conduct is the most important function of the system, and the failure of law enforcement to put criminality under tight control leads to the breakdown of public order. Accordingly, the system, in order to operate successfully, has to produce high rates of apprehension and conviction. A system operating under such conditions places a high premium on speed and results: legal facts are established quickly during police interrogation, prosecutorial review of the facts, and even cross-examination in court. Such a system operates under the presumption of guilt rather than innocence. The determination that there is sufficient evidence of guilt is sometimes made in the earliest stages of judicial processing—the police investigation stage—and all subsequent actions directed against the suspect continue to be based on this assumption. This approach can be described in terms of "diminishing presumption of innocence" which in many cases represents nothing more than an aggregation of attitudes, stereotypes, and the surrounding mood in the community (or entire society), as well as in the criminal justice system.

In contrast, the due process model often takes on the appearance of an obstacle course in which each successive stage is designed to present formidable impediments to carrying the accused any further along the judicial process. The due process model is far more committed to the formal structure of the legal system; to a large extent, it relies on nonadjudicative fact-finding, the possibility of error being emphasized at all stages. The operative assumption can be linked to quality control, as in a factory production line, where much of the input is devoted to the quality of the products and not necessarily to the quantitative aspect of the output. The dominant doctrine of the model is commitment to the notion of legal guilt. According to this doctrine, a person cannot be held guilty on the basis of probable cause. Guilt is determined in the process of legal procedures performed by the authorities acting within the framework of their allocated competencies.

In attempting to account for disparities, unequal treatment, or discrimination within a given society, neither model seems to be adequate on its own. It seems, at least in Israel, that the disparities found between Jews and Arabs can be attributed to the fact that the two models operate simultaneously within the same system. Neither of them, however, is applied in its ideal typical form. The control model is not totally blind to legal evidence and facts, nor is it divorced from the context of due process which constitutes the prescribed model of the Israeli criminal justice system. However, the fact that the system is consistently less lenient towards Arabs (they have a lower probability, over all of having their files closed, a higher probability of being convicted, and a greater likelihood of being sentenced to a term in prison) might suggest that stereotypes and extralegal considerations tend to overshadow the principle of due process when the suspect is an Arab. Being an Arab may lead to a presumption of guilt regardless of facts and the rules of evidence—as in the control model.

Intervention by the criminal justice system is not applied equally across the various social classes and population groups of society. Any such practice would evoke public outcry and promptly bring it to a halt. Thus, the danger lies in the discriminatory enforcement of the law among the weaker elements of the population—the poor, the weak, and members of minority groups. These elements are the least capable of drawing attention to their plight, and their suffering usually goes unheeded by the vast majority of the population. Under such circumstances, if the discriminatory conduct of the criminal justice system appears to be a legitimized norm, it is hardly surprising that respect for the law in marginal groups is often eroded.

The first stage in processing an individual through the criminal justice system involves opening a police file. This may involve just a technical-procedural act, followed by a police investigation (with or without detention). The initiation of police intervention and the opening of a file against an individual normally takes place when certain facts implicate the individual and turn him into a suspect. A police file is seldom opened, nor are other legal steps usually taken, in the absence of specific implicating facts. Such practices of proactive enforcement are more typical of the control model. If, indeed, members of a certain ethnic or socioeconomic group are exposed to higher levels of criminal justice activity (i.e., more arrests, charges, and convictions), then we can say, in the quantitative language of Donald Black (1976), that "more law" or "more policing" is being exercised. This has led to the assumption that the law and other modes of social control will be imposed differentially and, in this sense, "more law" will be imposed on the weaker elements of society.

During the period covered by our study (1980–1992), the general crime statistics in Israel never reached the critical level for the crime problem, nor did society's reaction to it feature high on the public agenda. On the contrary, although the general crime rate in Israel increased in a linear fashion from 28 per one thousand population in 1951–1952 to 53.2 per one thousand in 1995 (a 190% increase), in the 1980s there was a decline—the general crime rate decreased from 61.2 police files per one thousand population in 1981 to 52.3 in 1990. Until 1995, the total increase in the crime rate was less than 0.2 percent (53.2 per one thousand). Overall, this reflects a quite stable picture of criminality—not one that could be perceived as alarming. These rates are not indicative of a control model ideology that governs the law enforcement policy. Moreover, there was virtually no change in the offender rate in the Israeli-Arab sector (16 offenders per one thousand population in 1981, and 17.7 in 1992). Hence, one cannot point at Israeli Arabs as the core of the crime problem in Israel, and there is no numerical evidence to explain why Arabs are often more harshly treated by the criminal justice system in its "war against crime."

"JUDGE RIGHTEOUSLY"—JEWS AND ISRAELI ARABS

The high visibility of "Arab crime" leads to the stereotyping of Arabs in general. Due to their high involvement in violent and security offenses, they are considered by many as constituting a risk group. It is very hard to distinguish between the cause and effect of this stigmatization process. Is the high conviction rate of Arabs in these crime categories a result of objectively more frequent involvement, or do higher levels of law enforcement action (control) drive the detection and conviction process? Clearly, criminal statistics tend to substantiate what is already "known" and reinforce existing stereotypes, such as "Arabs as a fifth column." Our discussion in chapter 2 showed that Arabs, more than members of other ethnic groups, are perceived as criminals who commit more violent crimes. It is quite likely that being considered a "high risk" group by large parts of the public affects criminal justice officials such as police officers, prosecutors, and judges who, after all, are also members of the public. It is suggested here that such perceptions and beliefs may, consciously or subconsciously, affect the decision making of a system—a system that requires decisions at every juncture.

Our data clearly show overrepresentation of file closure among Arabs (39%, relative to their 22% share in the total number of files opened). Had the decision not to prosecute (file closure) been completely random, the closure rate would have been about 22 percent. The fact that the file closure rate is much higher (by more than 77%) shows that the system tends to close Arab files beyond randomness. This trend holds true across all crime categories. However, no conclusion regarding discrimination or lack of it can be made from this finding without conducting a more detailed analysis of the data. Comparison between Arabs and Jews (in the multivariate analysis) produced inconclusive results, thus excluding the possibility of arriving at any conclusion regarding discriminatory practices. Beyond nationality, which is an extralegal variable, criminal history also plays a significant role in the decision to close a file, previous criminal record increasing the probability of having to stand trial.

A quite different picture is conveyed by our findings on conviction, where the discrepancies between Jews and Arabs seem to grow—across all offenses, the probability of an Arab defendant with no prior criminal history being convicted was found to be 1.6 times higher than that of a Jewish defendant with the same profile. This ratio is maintained for all other profiles, and when the overall likelihood of being convicted is higher. For instance, the probability of a forty five-year-old Arab defendant with no prior criminal record being convicted is 1.6 times higher than that of a Jewish defendant with the same profile. The magnitude of this discrepancy is maintained consistently throughout the analysis, across specific crime categories such as violent, public order, and property offenses.

In addition to the overall comparison between Jews and Arabs, a time dimension was also introduced into our analysis. The data show a significant difference in the probability of file closure and conviction between the early and latter periods of our study. In comparing the first and last periods covered by our study (1980–1981) and (1990–1992), we found that the earlier period seems to have produced less lenient outcomes with regard to file closure. The two periods do not differ in the tendency to open police files. On the contrary, it can be argued that the rate of files opened actually lagged behind the increase in the population size—in fact, the crime rates (measured by the number of files opened per 100,000) actually went down. This makes it even more difficult to explain why more file closure takes place in the early 1990s than in the early 1980s. From examination of the rate of criminal incidents, the police were clearly under no particular pressure to be more "productive." However, this does not mean that the number of offenders also remained stable. The findings can perhaps be explained by two factors which, at first glance, might seem unrelated. First, prosecutorial screening has, in general, shifted more towards a due process model in the sense that more emphasis is placed on principles such as the rule of evidence. The application of more stringent criteria makes it more difficult to substantiate a case sufficiently to warrant criminal prosecution. Second, changes in the features of criminal events may not be reflected in increased offender rates. Following the Intifada, more crimes against the public order were reported. In such crimes, and also in certain other violent offenses, especially in the case of riots and disturbances of the peace, large numbers of suspects may be booked by the police and sometimes even detained. Thus, with no increase in the number of criminal events, we obtain an increase in the number of offenders—opening of files. However, due to the stringent requirements of the prosecution, many of such suspects are set free and the charges against them dropped for lack of concrete evidence; hence, the increase in the file closure rate in the 1990s.

This trend is paired with another finding; namely, the increase in the conviction rate in the 1990s compared to the early 1980s. By now, this phenomenon should be almost self-explanatory. Careful scrutiny of police files prior to a decision to seek prosecution increases the likelihood of conviction. Thus, we see that in the latter period of our study (1990–1992), there is a dramatic increase in the likelihood of file closure and, at the same time, a significant increase in the probability of conviction.

Finally, after conviction, we examined the likelihood of receiving a prison sentence. The most striking finding in this stage of the analysis is that criminal history is the best predictor of whether a prison sentence is imposed on a convicted offender. However, the nationality of the convicted offender also plays a significant role in the prison sentence decision. Controlling for all other variables, the estimated probability of a prison sentence being imposed on an Arab is 1.6 times higher than that of a Jew. This discrepancy is even larger in the category of violent offenses.

It should be noted that beyond the effect of nationality, other variables such as age, family status, and criminal history also play a significant role in the decision to send a convicted criminal to prison. In general, younger offenders are more likely (sometimes twice as likely) than older offenders to be sentenced to prison. A similar trend is identifiable with regard to family status—unmarried offenders are more likely to be sentenced to prison than married offenders.

OUR PALESTINIAN NEIGHBORS: THE STRANGERS IN OUR MIDST

The lives of Palestinian Arabs in the West Bank and Gaza Strip have been affected in many ways by the Israeli occupation. The opening of the borders with Israel turned the Palestinian Arabs into a labor-exporting society. However, unlike migrant workers from other labor-exporting societies, Palestinian Arabs were not uprooted from their social and cultural context; they simply became a commuting labor force participating in a booming Israeli economy in chronic need of cheap labor. The new labor opportunities that opened up to the Palestinians had tremendous impact, not only on the high unemployment rates in the West Bank and Gaza Strip, but also on social and cultural aspects of Palestinian life. Palestinian Arabs became exposed to a modern western society; employment in Israel contributed to a huge increase in their earnings which, in turn, was immediately translated into changes in lifestyle and redistribution of wealth. Another by-product of exposure to the modern Israeli society was rebellion against traditional cultural norms. The most visible aspect of anti-traditional conduct was the adoption of new dress codes and recreational patterns. Changes also occurred on the normative level with regard to conduct towards family members, the elderly, and the acceptance of parental control and discipline. All in all, there was a weakening in the strength of religion and tradition which, prior to the occupation, had played a central role in what had essentially been a peasant society. Exposure to western society on the one hand, and the decline of traditional values, opened the door to negative developments. Israeli-Palestinian cooperation became a feature of illegal drug traffic, car theft, buying and selling stolen property, and other criminal activities. Thus, Palestinians learned how to benefit from both the legal and illegal opportunities that opened up to them due to the proximity and strong economic ties that developed with Israel. For many Israelis, the perception of the Palestinian Arab was that of a low-paid, unskilled manual laborer, as well as a car thief or even a potential terrorist seeking opportunities to plant bombs and kill Jews; in general, a highly untrustworthy individual.

To the best of our knowledge, no study has documented the criminogenic potential embedded in the relationship between Palestinian and Israeli society. The complex political and social milieu, described here and in chapter 6, led us to hypothesize, on the one hand, that the criminal justice system could hardly fail to be influenced by prevailing stereotypes and, on the other, that Palestinian criminals would be treated in a discriminatory manner by the Israeli legal authorities.

Our findings corroborate some of our concerns—the data clearly confirm the common Israeli belief that Palestinians present a security threat and therefore are treated more harshly by the criminal justice system. Analysis of the general model (all crime categories) shows that the chance of a Palestinian suspect having his file closed is indeed smaller than that of his Jewish counterpart. However, the effect of nationality on the decision to close a police file washes out completely in certain specific crime categories. In the three major categories (violent, public order, and property offenses), being a Palestinian has no statistically significant effect on the likelihood of file closure. Comparison of Jews and Palestinians fails to show evidence of discrimination against Palestinians in the decision to prosecute. On the other hand, a different, and quite unexpected picture is obtained when the comparison is made between Palestinians and Israeli Arabs. The general model does not enable conclusions to be drawn about differential treatment, but when public order offenses are examined, Palestinians have a significantly better chance of having their files closed than their Israeli Arab brethren. The nature of the criminal events in which Palestinian Arabs are involved may lead to mass arrests (including arrests of Palestinians within the borders of the state of Israel); hence, the higher rates of file closure following police investigation.

A somewhat different picture is obtained with regard to convictions. In general, we find that both Jews and Arabs have a higher chance of being convicted than Palestinians. This holds true across time, from the first period of the study (1980–1982) to the last period (1990–1992). However, examination by specific offense categories (violent, property, and public order offenses) reveals that Palestinians have a higher probability of being convicted compared to Jews and Israeli Arabs, even though some of the discrepancies are quite small and, in some cases, the Israeli Arabs are the ones with a higher chance of being convicted.

In the sentencing stage, it appears that Palestinians are perceived as even more of a threat: comparison of the estimated likelihood of receiving a prison sentence showed that Palestinian Arabs had a higher probability of receiving a prison sentence on every single profile, especially in comparison to Jewish offenders. It should be noted that apart from nationality, criminal history also plays a significant role in the decision to impose a prison sentence; the chances of receiving a prison sentence increase even further the more serious the criminal history.

BEYOND NUMBERS AND STATISTICS

In a 1987 government resolution to provide special benefits for Druze and Circassian citizens (two small ethnic minority groups in Israel known for their loyalty to the state), the government conceded that these two ethnic minorities had not enjoyed true equality with the Jewish sector, but in the same breath, it announced that the principle of equality would not be applied to the entire Arab community in Israel. To those who are familiar with the long list of domains in which institutional discrimination has taken place over the years, this might not be interpreted as alarming or even surprising. Discriminatory practices have been well documented in many public and institutional areas, from the allocation of governmental and municipal budgets and resources, to public housing, education, land appropriation, and much more. Our study has documented, perhaps for the first time, the existence of discrimination against Arabs in the criminal justice system. The findings of the aggregated data leave no room for doubt that the decisions made at each stage of the criminal procedure discriminate against Arabs (both Israeli Arabs and Palestinians). The fact that this conclusion is based on the findings of a multivariate analysis of more than sixty thousand cases over a period of more than a decade clearly puts paid to any argument that the discrepancies are a consequence of the whims of individual criminal justice officials. It is conceivable that differential treatment of Jews and Arabs in other public areas such as budgetary allocations, housing, and land appropriation can be attributed to governmental policy and legislation. Differential decisions regarding arrest, file closure, conviction, and sentencing are not necessarily the end result of policy or intention.

Ever since the turn of the century, the deep cleavage between Jews and Arabs has left residues of mistrust and even hatred towards the Arab population. This sense of alienation finds a degree of legitimation in the fact that the Declaration of Independence left no doubt as to the Jewish identity of the new state of Israel. Many other countries have national and ethnic minorities, but the model adopted here is different—pursuing the goal of the Zionist movement to establish a home for the Jewish people, Israel was established and constitutionally defined as a Jewish state. As we saw in our early discussion on Jews and Arabs, the Arab minority living in Israel became party to the endless conflict of the Arab countries with Israel—they were citizens of a state that was constantly at war with their own Arab brethren. This situation, perhaps, provided the justification for the underlying functional need (for some, almost an ideology) to control this potentially threatening group by discriminatory practices. Only in this way can we explain how one and the same Supreme Court could rescind legitimacy from a political party calling for the degradation of Arabs and the denial of their political rights and, at the same time, refuse to intervene in a policy decision denying Arabs the right to purchase housing accommodations in east Jerusalem, an area formerly populated by Arabs (see chapter 1 for a discussion of the Bourkan decision). Israel is a society committed to equal rights for all citizens, irrespective of race and nationality. However, for the duration of its short history, it has lived with a threatening minority in its midst, one which has been consistently subjected to overt and covert discriminatory practices. Moreover, the "covert" discrimination revealed by the findings of our study is probably not limited to formal agencies such as the criminal justice system, but traceable in many varied and diffuse social systems.

It is commonly believed that the legal system is a mirror of the entire society. However, in the case of Israeli society, it is hard to determine whether the courts mirror the national mood or whether, perhaps, the national mood reflects the legal system. Research conducted by Smooha (1996) found that the majority (74.1%) of Jews in Israel would grant preferential treatment to Jews if given the opportunity. A more recent national survey of 565 Jews found that 56 percent concurred with the proposition that Arab citizens should be denied the right to elect the country's prime minister (*Ha'aretz*, August 21, 1977). It is suggested here that a criminal justice system that functions in such a hostile environment will probably be ready to tolerate discrimination against members of the Arab minority. Under such circumstances, many members of the Arab community are likely to develop a deep sense of injustice, as is, indeed, shown in our survey.

Analysis of our survey data suggests that dissatisfaction with the criminal justice system is expressed by a higher level of perceived injustice among Arabs than among Jews. It is clear from the findings of our longitudinal study that Arabs, as members of a national minority, suffer injustice to a much larger extent than Jews. The degree of perceived injustice expressed by the subjects of our attitudinal survey is linked to an important component of the criminal justice system; namely, compliance. It is clear from the responses to our survey that negative experiences lead to more readiness to violate the rules, even at the cost of being caught and punished. This model applies to the entire population, but even more so to Arabs, whose sense of perceived injustice is much stronger; hence, their greater readiness to take the law into their own hands, and their tendency to justify such action on ideological grounds.

THE CRIMINAL JUSTICE SYSTEM IN THE TWENTY-FIRST CENTURY

As we approach the new millennium and the fiftieth anniversary of the establishment of the state of Israel, let us attempt to take a look into the future and see what it holds in store for us. Israel's population has grown by 900 percent since it establishment. Its ethnic and cultural diversity has been maintained, and the pains of resettlement continue to accompany the waves of immigration. Israel's growth in size and diversity undoubtedly has beneficial outcomes for society. However, it also has a downside which is reflected in alienation, social disorder, unemployment, and crime. The recent immigration from the former Soviet Union, for instance, has changed the demographic composition of Israel's prison population—one-third of the inmates currently imprisoned are from the former Soviet Union, especially the Islamic Republics. The crime scene is also changing—more violence, including domestic violence, and more organized crime (racketeering, extortion, prostitution) are revealed by the police statistics. Size, per se, has affected Israeli society—the previously small and cohesive community has become more of a "Gesellschaft," in which formal sanctions are more appropriate than informal means of social control in regulating behavior and maintaining the law and order.

Property crime, much of it related to drugs, and an alarmingly high rate of vehicle theft currently dominate the crime scene, forming a major concern among citizens. There is no reason to expect the crime rate to go down in the future. On the contrary, it is more plausible to expect an increase in crime as the society grows in size and density.

The geopolitical situation also has its input to the crime scene. If the peace process picks up again, and economic collaboration develops, criminal collaboration should also be expected. More relaxed border controls and closer ties between the Israeli and Palestinian economies will make Israel a preferred target for property offenses by Palestinians due to the disparities in wealth between the two neighboring societies.

Such a scenario actually portrays Israel as a normal, heterogeneous society, with a relatively high population density. Close to 90 percent of the population is concentrated in urban centers and about 45 percent reside in the large urban conglomerate formed by Tel-Aviv—the business and commercial capital of Israel—and its sprawling suburbs. Under such conditions, and with the growing accumulation of wealth by Israelis, pressure will grow on government to provide better protection for its citizens, and to be more efficient in fighting crime. The role of the judiciary in a free and liberal society is clear. Fighting discrimination and injustice is a primary function of the system. At a time of increasing crime rates, public outcry, and demands on police efficiency, the criminal justice system will be under pressure to apprehend, prosecute, and convict offenders. The question that arises is, who will become the targets of the law enforcement agencies? And, no less important, how will the civil and legal rights of the clients be guaranteed? Such demands for "more law" may lead to overemphasis of the crime control model at the expense of due process. Public fear of property and violent crime often leads to stereotyped definitions of the "dangerous elements" in society in much the same way that the poor, unemployed, and African Americans in the United States are viewed as "dangerous elements" hence forming the target of law enforcement efforts. Based on past experience, it can be assumed that in Israel, too, the target of law enforcement efforts will be the weaker social elements and members of minority groups.

The current study has alerted us to existing discrepancies in the outputs of the criminal justice system. It has revealed discriminatory practices which cannot be discerned by observing individual cases. When all the cases are aggregated and looked at from a macro perspective, we obtained a very disturbing "bird's-eye view" of the situation—one that has to serve as a warning sign of what may lie in store for us in the future. If more crime, social unrest, alienation, and wider economic gaps lie ahead, there will also be more pressure and demands on the agents of law enforcement for greater efficiency. It is therefore important to ensure that greater efficiency be balanced by strengthening the guardians of the rule of law—the judicial system and especially the courts—in order to protect civil rights and due process, thereby securing freedom and equality for all citizens as stated in the Declaration of Independence of the state of Israel in 1948.

Appendix

Appendix Table 1
Logistic Regression for Conviction: General Model

Variable	Parameter Estimate	Standard Error	Wald Chi-Square	pr > Wald χ^2
Intercept	-2.7462	0.068	1594.1654	0.0001
Arab	0.641	0.032	403.637	0.0001
Recidivism	-0.0615	0.0116	28.2713	0.0001
Age	0.0482	0.00116	850.2718	0.0001
Family Status	0.5299	0.0286	344.0489	0.0001
Prior Prison Sentence	0.6173	0.0449	189.2054	0.0001
Prior Convictions	0.0947	0.0038	601.6645	0.0001
Sex	-0.4763	0.039	146.8469	0.0001
Period 2	2.0346	0.0480	1799.0185	0.0001
Period 3	2.1532	0.0423	2594.1819	0.0001
Period 4	2.3660	0.0413	3283.62.02	0.0001
Period 5	2.4272	0.0410	3506.0329	0.0001
Period 6	2.8123	0.0469	3591.7661	0.0001

Appendix Table 2
Logistic Regression for Conviction: Violent Offenses

Variable	Parameter Estimate	Standard Error	Wald Chi-Square	pr > Wald χ^2
Intercept	-2.5002	0.1767	200.1447	0.0001
Arab	0.7338	0.0834	77.3500	0.0001
Recidivism	0.0696	0.0328	4.4930	0.0001
Age	0.0363	0.00379	91.4729	0.0001
Family Status	0.3475	0.0748	29.5961	0.0001
Prior Prison Sentence	0.1606	0.1546	1.07801	N.S.
Prior Convictions	0.0593	0.0141	17.7956	0.0001
Sex	-0.5431	0.1052	26.6619	0.0001
Period 2	2.2523	0.1297	301.4936	0.0001
Period 3	2.4016	0.1194	404.5929	0.0001
Period 4	2.1800	0.1109	386.2694	0.0001
Period 5	2.5146	0.1114	509.2764	0.0001
Period 6	2.6044	0.1182	485.5055	0.0001

Appendix Table 3
Logistic Regression for Conviction: Public Order Offenses

Variable	Parameter Estimate	Standard Error	Wald Chi-Square	pr > Wald χ^2
Intercept	-1.7736	0.1299	186.5081	0.0001
Arab	0.6479	0.0679	91.1558	0.0001
Recidivism	-0.1125	0.0248	20.5231	0.0001
Age	0.0272	0.00310	77.2946	0.0001
Family Status	0.4826	0.0601	64.3736	0.0001
Prior Prison Sentence	0.5980	0.1134	27.8035	0.0001
Prior Convictions	0.0898	0.0101	79.4370	0.0001
Sex	-0.5326	0.0759	49.1973	0.0001
Period 2	1.9146	0.1087	310.2834	0.0001
Period 3	2.0442	0.0922	491.9649	0.0001
Period 4	2.1953	0.0879	623.5038	0.0001
Period 5	2.4404	0.0931	687.5080	0.0001
Period 6	2.6044	0.1182	485.5055	0.0001

Appendix Table 4
Logistic Regression for Conviction: Property Offenses

Variable	Parameter Estimate	Standard Error	Wald Chi-Square	pr > Wald χ^2
Intercept	-3.6570	0.1319	768.4910	0.0001
Arab	0.6443	0.0487	175.3474	0.0001
Recidivism	-0.0287	0.0182	2.5015	N.S.
Age	0.0779	0.00350	496.5461	0.0001
Family Status	0.6525	0.0469	193.5292	0.0001
Prior Prison Sentence	0.9213	0.0676	185.55312	0.0001
Prior Convictions	0.1113	0.00590	356.3198	0.0001
Sex	-0.5105	0.0762	44.8647	0.0001
Period 2	2.0111	0.0746	726.7112	0.0001
Period 3	2.0533	0.0677	919.1277	0.0001
Period 4	2.3985	0.0669	1286.9395	0.0001
Period 5	2.4063	0.0674	1275.8126	0.0001
Period 6	2.7922	0.0794	1235.2933	0.0001

Bibliography

Alport, G. W., and L. J. Postman (1947). *The psychology of rumor*. New York: Henry Holt.

Barak, A. (1986). *The rule of law*. Unpublished proceedings from lectures to judges.

———. (1993) *Protected human rights: Range and limits*. In *Constitutional law*, Baruch Beracha and Ariel Ben Dor, eds. Faculty of Law University of Haifa. (In Hebrew)

Biafora, F. A., G. J. Warheit, R.S. Zimerman, A.G. Gil, E.A. Apospori, W.A. Vega, and D.L. Taylor (1993). Cultural mistrust and deviant behaviors among ethnically diverse black adolescent boys. *Journal of Applied Social Psychology* 23: 891–910.

Bin-Nun, A. (1992). *The law of the state of Israel: An introduction*. Jerusalem: Rubin Mass. Ltd.

Black, D. (1976). *The behavior of law*. New York: Academic Press.

Blumstein, A. (1982). On racial disproportionality of United States prison populations. *Journal of Criminal Law and Criminology* 73: 1259–1281.

Bonger, W. A. (1969)[1916]. *Criminality and economic conditions* (A.T. Turk, abr.). Bloomington: Indiana University Press.

Bottoms, A. E. (1983). *Neglected features of a contemporary penal system*. In *The power to punish,* David Garland and Peter Young, eds. London: Heinemann Educational Books.

Brislin, R. W. (1981). *Cross cultural encounters*. New York: Pergamon.

Bullock, H. A. (1961). Significance of the racial factor in the length of prison sentence. *Journal of Criminal Law, Criminology and Police Science* 52: 411–417.

Cohen, B. Z. (1981). *Jewish and Arab offenders in Israel: A study of ethnicity, class and minority experience*. Ph.D. Thesis, Bryn Mawr College.

———. (1985). Judicial discretion and sentencing disparity in adult felony courts in Israel. *Journal of Criminal Justice* 13: 99–115.

———, and S. Palmor (1985). The impact of ethnicity on probation recommendation and disposition in Israel. *Justice Quarterly* 2(2): 197–212.

Cohen, S. (1989). *Crime, justice and social control in the Israeli Arab population*. Tel Aviv: International Center for Peace in the Middle East.

Dahrendorf, R. (1959). *Class and class conflict in industrial society*. Stanford, CA: Stanford University Press.

Dixon, J. (1995). The organizational context of criminal sentencing. *American Journal of*

Sociology 100 (5): 1157–1198.

Farnworth, M., R. Teske, and G. Thruman (1991). *Ethnic, racial and minority disparity in felony court processing*. In *Race and criminal justice*, p. 54–70, M. J. Lynch and E. B. Patterson, eds. New York: Harrow and Heston.

Fishman G. (1983). On war and crime. In *Stress in Israel*, p. 165–180, S. Breznitz ed. New York: Van Nostrand Reinhold Company.

———, and M. Argov (1980). Crime trends in Israel 1951-1976. *Delinquency and Social Deviance* 1980: 25-35. (In Hebrew)

———, A. Rattner, and G. Weimann (1987). The effect of ethnicity on crime attribution. *Criminology* 25(3): 507–523.

———, and J. Soroka (1980). The impact of legal and extralegal factors on judicial decisions. *Society and Welfare* 1980:147-161.

Frishtik, M. (1983). *The relative importance of four alternative models in judging young adults aged 18-21 in the Israeli courts*. Unpublished Ph.D. Thesis, Bar-Ilan University. (In Hebrew)

Gabison, R. (1987). A very sad prognosis. *Politics* 16: 6. (In Hebrew)

———. (1991). *Administrative discretion in law enforcement*. The Center For Legislative Research and Comparative Law, Faculty of Law, Hebrew University, Jerusalem. (In Hebrew)

George-Abeyie, D. (1984). *The criminal justice system and blacks*. New York: Clark Boardman.

Gibson, J. L. (1978). Race as a determinant of criminal sentences: a methodological critique and case study. *Law & Society Review* 12: 455–478.

Gillespie, R. W. (1980). Fines as an alternative to incarceration: the German experience. *Federal Probation* 44(4): 20–26.

Golomb, N. (1992). *Two volumes of sentencing*. Tel-Aviv: Naftali Golomb.

Ha'aretz (daily newspaper in Hebrew). (1989). A New car for 500 N.I.S. January 12, p.13.

———. (1997). Jews deny Arabs' rights. August 21, p. 8.

Hagan, J. (1974). Extra legal attributes and criminal sentencing: An assessment of a sociological viewpoint. *Law & Society Review* 8: 357.

———, and C. Albonetti (1982). Race, class, and the perception of criminal injustice in America. *American Journal of Sociology* 88: 329–355.

———, and K. Bumiller (1983). Making sense of sentencing: a review and critique of sentencing research. In *Research in sentencing: The search for reform*. Blumstein, A. J. Cohen, S. E. Martin, and M. H. Tonry, eds. Washington, D.C.: National Academy of Science.

———, and R. D. Peterson (1984). Changing conceptions of race: towards an account of anomalous findings of sentencing research. *American Sociological Review* 49: 70.

Haj Yihieh, M., G. Rahav, and M. Teichman (1994). The municipal court and its functioning with Arabs in Israel. *Pelilim* IV: 157–173. (In Hebrew)

Hassin, Y. (1987). The recidivist criminal, the dangerous criminal, and criminal career. *Crime and Social Deviance* (1–2): 5-18. (In Hebrew)

———, and M. Kremnitzer (1988). Uniformity and sentence in traffic offenses. *Mishpatim* 18(1). (In Hebrew).

Holmes, M.D., H. M. Hosch, H. C. Daudistel, D. A. Perez, and J. B. Graves (1996). Ethnicity, legal resources and felony dispositions in two jurisdictions. *Justice Quarterly* 13(1):11-30.

Horowitz, D., and M. Lisak (1989). *Trouble in utopia*. Albany: State University of New York Press.

Huff, C. R., A. Rattner, and E. Sagarin (1996). *Convicted but innocent: Wrongful conviction and public policy*. Thousand Oaks: Sage Publications.

Israel Central Bureau of Statistics (1974). *Criminal statistics, 1974*. Special series No. 541.

———. (1978). *Judicial statistics 1978*. Special series No. 617.

———. (1992). *Criminal statistics 1992*. Special series No. 988.

———. (1996). *Judicial statistics 1996*. Special series No. 1031.

Israel National Police. *Annual report, 1991; 1996*.

Israel Prison Service (1970). Department of Corrections. *Annual report 1970*.

———. (1988). Department of Corrections. *Annual report 1987/88*.

Johnson, G. (1941). The negro and crime. *American Academy of Political and Social Sciences* 271: 93–104.

Joreskog, K. G., and D. Sorbom. (1993). *Lisrel 8 and Prelis*. Chicago: Scientific Software International, Inc.

Kimmerling, B., and J. S. Migdal (1993). *Palestinians—The making of the people*. New York: Free Press.

Kleck, G. (1981). Racial discrimination in criminal sentencing: a critical evaluation of the evidence with additional evidence on the death penalty. *American Sociological Review 46* (December): 783–805.

Klein, S., J. Petersilia, and S. Turner (1990). Race and imprisonment decisions in California. *Science* 247: 812–816.

Kramer, H. J., and J. T. Ulmer (1996). Sentencing disparity and departures from guidelines. *Justice Quarterly* 13(1):81-106.

Kretzmer, D. (1990). *The legal status of the Arabs in Israel*. Boulder, CO: Westview Press.

LaFree, G. D. (1985). Official reactions to Hispanic defendants in the southwest. *Journal of Research in Crime and Delinquency 22*:213–37.

Loftus, E. F., and J. C. Palmer (1974). Reconstruction of automobile destruction: an example of Interaction between language and memory. *Journal of Verbal Learning and Verbal Behavior* 13: 585–589.

Lukacs, G. (1971). *History and class consciousness*. Cambridge, MA: MIT Press.

Lynch, M. J., and W. B. Groves (1989). The correlates of crime: a critique of causal and methodological issues. Paper presented at the Annual meeting of the American Society of Criminology, November, Reno, Nevada.

Lynch, M. J., and B. E. Patterson, eds. (1991). *Race and criminal Justice*. New York: Harrow and Haston.

Marx, K. (1859). *A contribution to the critique of political economy*. New York: Vintage.

Montagu, A. (1964). *The concept of race*. New York: Macmillan.

Myers, M. A., and S. Talerico (1987). *The social context of criminal sentencing*. New York: Springer Verlag.

Nelson, J. F. (1994). A dollar a day: sentencing misdemeanants in New York State. *Journal of Research of Crime and Delinquency* 31(2): 183-201.

Nirel R., S. F. Landau, L. Sebba, and B. Sagiv (1997). The effectiveness of service work: an analysis of recidivism. *Journal of Quantitative Criminology* 13(1): 73–92.

Packer, H. L. (1968). *The limits of the criminal sanction*. Stanford, CA: Stanford University Press.

Palestinian Central Bureau of Statistics (1996). *Survey of households victimization.* Palestinian Authority.

Palmor, S. (1982). *The offender's nationality as a factor in the probation officer's recommendation and the sentencing decision*. M.A. Thesis, Department of Social Work, University of Haifa. (In Hebrew).

Peretz, D. (1988). *Israel and the Palestinian Arabs*. Washington, D.C.: Middle Eastern Instiute.

Petersilia, J. (1983). *Racial disparities in the criminal justice system*. Santa Monica, CA: Rand Corporation.

Pope, C. E. (1976). The influence of social and legal factors on sentence dispositions: a preliminary analysis of offender-based transaction statistics. *Journal of Criminal Justice* 4: 203–221.

Rattner, A. (1994). The margins of justice, attitudes towards the law and the legal system among Jews and Arabs in Israel. *International Journal of Public Opinion Research* 6(4): 358-370.

———. (1996). The effect of legal and extralegal variables on sentencing in Israel. *Justice Quarterly* (13)1:129-149.

Reifen, D. (1966). A comparative study of Jewish and Arab juvenile delinquents in Israel. *Delinquency and Society* 1. (In Hebrew)

Schmeltz, U., and D. Salzman (1962;1964). *Criminal statistics in Israel 1949-1958, Volume I, Tables, 1962; Volume II, Analysis, 1964*. Publications of the Institute of Criminology, the Hebrew University of Jerusalem.

Sellin, T. (1928). The Negro criminal: A statistical note. *Annals of the American Academy of Political and Social Science* 52.

Simon, R. J. (1989). Israel confidence in social institutions and beliefs about democracy. Unpublished manuscript in Crime, justice and social control in the Israeli Arab population, S. Cohen, Tel-Aviv: International Center for Peace in the Middle East.

———, and J. M. Landis (1990). Trends in public support for civil liberties and due process in Israeli society. *Social Science Quarterly* 71(1): 93-104.

Smooha, S. (1996). Ethic democracy: Israel as an archtype. In *Zionism: Contemporary debate*. Beer-Sheva: Ben-Gurion Center.

Spohn, C., and J. Cederblom (1991). Race and disparities in sentencing: A test of the liberation hypothesis. *Justice Quarterly* 8(3): 305–27.

Spohn, C., J. Gruhl, and S. Welch (1981-82). The effect of race on sentencing: A reexamination of an unsettled question. *Law and Society Review* 16(1): 72-88.

Taylor, L. D., F. A. Biafora, Jr., and G. Warheit (1994). Racial mistrust among immigrants. *Social Problems* (85): 1923-39.

Terrell, F. (1980). *The development of an inventory to measure certain aspects of cultural mistrust among Blacks*. Paper presented at the Fifth Conference on Empirical Research in Black Psychology, Washington, DC: Howard University.

———, S. Terrell, and J. Taylor (1981). Effects of race of examiner and cultural mistrust on the WAIS performance of black students. *Journal of Consulting Clinical Psychology* 49: 750-751.

Tyler, T. (1990). *Why people obey the law*. New Haven and London: Yale University Press.

Zatz, M. S. (1984). Race, ethnicity, and determinate sentencing: A new dimension to an old controversy. *Criminology* 22(2): 147-171.

Zureik, E. T. (1991). Two years of the Intifada: A statistical profile of Palestinian victims. *Third World Quarterly* 12(3-4): 97-123.

———, and F. Moughrabi, eds. (1988). *Different scales of justice: Arabs and Jews in Israel—Results of a national survey*. Near East Cultural and Educational Foundation of Canada and International Center for Research and Public Policy.

Index

About the Authors

ARYE RATTNER is Professor of Sociology at the University of Haifa. He has written numerous articles on wrongful conviction and eyewitness identification and is coauthor of the book *Convicted But Innocent: Wrongful Conviction and Public Policy* (1996).

GIDEON FISHMAN is Professor of Sociology at the University of Haifa. He is co-founder and co-director of the Minerva Center for Youth Policy at the University. He is the author of numerous articles on crime trends, stereotypes, violent behavior, and suicidal behavior.

ISBN 0-275-95908-2
90000>
EAN
9 780275 959081
HARDCOVER BAR CODE